ROUGH GUIDES

POCKET **ROUGH GUIDE**
LISBON

written and researched by
MATTHEW HANCOCK

CONTENTS

LISBON

Set across a series of hills overlooking the broad estuary of the Rio Tejo (River Tagus), Lisbon's stunning location and effortless beauty immediately strike most first-time visitors. It's an instantly likeable place, a big city, with a population of around two million, but one that remains human enough in pace and scale to be easily taken in over a long weekend. That said, many visitors visit again and again, smitten by a combination of old-world charm and cosmopolitan vibrancy that makes it one of Europe's most exciting cities.

View of Lisbon from Cristo Rei

What's new

Lisbon's popularity continues to surge, as do its attractions. The Museum of Art, Architecture and Technology (see page 87) has become one of the riverside's most spectacular buildings, while the impressive Ponte 25 de Abril suspension bridge (see page 77) now has a lofty viewing platform and exhibition space. New to this guide is the Museu do Aljube (see page 37), which offers a fascinating insight into the harsh dictatorship of the Salazar regime up until the 1974 revolution.

Although one of the EU's least expensive capitals, Lisbon was once one of the continent's wealthiest, controlling a maritime empire that stretched from Brazil to Macau. The iconic Torre de Belém, Mosteiro dos Jerónimos and dramatic Moorish castle survive from these times, though many other buildings were destroyed in the Great Earthquake of 1755. Today, much of the historic centre – the Baixa, Chiado and Bairro Alto – dates from the late eighteenth and nineteenth centuries. The biggest attraction in these quarters is the street life: nothing beats watching the city's comings and goings from a pavement café over a powerful *bica* coffee or Portuguese beer.

If you're fit enough to negotiate its hills, Lisbon is a great place to explore on foot: get off the beaten track and you'll find atmospheric neighbourhoods sheltering aromatic *pastelarias* (patisseries), traditional shops, and shuttered houses faced with beautiful *azulejo* tiles. Getting around by public transport can be fun in itself, whether you're cranking uphill on one of the city's ancient trams, riding a ferry across the Rio Tejo, or speeding across town on the metro, whose stations are decorated with adventurous contemporary art.

Lisbon also boasts excellent museums – from the Gulbenkian, with its amazing collection of arts through the ages, to the Berardo, whose modern paintings are the envy of Europe, via the Museu Nacional de Arte Antiga, the national gallery, with top Portuguese and European masterpieces.

Lisbon's eclectic nightlife scene ranges from the traditional fado clubs of the Alfama district to glitzy venues in the Bairro Alto and along the riverfront, many of them playing African and Brazilian beats influenced by immigrants from Portugal's former colonies.

Elsewhere, the city offers a fascinating mishmash of the

Best places for alfresco dining

The best way to soak up Lisbon's atmosphere is to grab an outdoor table and sit back with a coffee or something more substantial. Sample tapas at *Pharmacia*, in a fine little garden overlooking the Tagus (see page 65), or enjoy a pizza-with-a-view at riverside *Casanova* (see page 46). It's hard to find a lovelier lunch spot than the sleek, riverside *À Margem* (see page 89). Alternatively, head to one of Lisbon's squares or *miradouros* (viewpoints), many of which have cafés, bars or restaurants, such as *Portas do Sol* (see page 49).

Portas do Sol restaurant

traditional and cutting edge: chequered-tiled bars full of old-timers supping brandies adjacent to boutiquey clubs pumping out the latest sounds; tiny *tascas* with bargain menus scrawled on boards rubbing shoulders with designer restaurants eyeing the latest Michelin awards, and tiny stores that wrap handmade products in paper and string overlooking gleaming shopping malls.

Should city life begin to pall, take the train out to the beautiful hilltop town of Sintra, whose lush wooded heights and royal palaces comprise a UNESCO World Heritage Site. Alternatively, the lively resorts of Estoril and Cascais are just half an hour away, with the best beaches lying south of the city, along the Costa da Caparica, where Atlantic breakers crash on kilometre after kilometre of superb dune-backed sands.

When to visit

Lisbon is comfortably warm from April to October (average daily temperature 20–28ºC), with cooling Atlantic breezes making it less hot than Mediterranean cities on the same latitude. Most Lisbon residents take their holidays in July and August (27–28ºC), which means that some shops, bars and restaurants close for the period and the local beaches are heaving. Lower temperatures of 22–26ºC mean September and October are good times to visit, as is June, when the city enjoys its main festivals. Even in midwinter it is rarely cold and, as one of Europe's sunniest capitals, the sun usually appears at some stage to light up the city.

Where to...

Shop

Suburban Lisbon has some of Europe's largest shopping malls, but the city centre is a pleasing mixture of quirky local stores and smaller independent outlets. The top end of **Avenida da Liberdade** features the likes of Armani and Louis Vuitton, while Chiado is the place to head for glass and jewellery. Antique shops cluster round **São Bento**, **Príncipe Real** and **Campo de Santa Clara**, while off-the-wall clothing and accessories are to be found in the independent boutiques of the **Bairro Alto**. **Santos** has become the district of design, with several stores dedicated to contemporary jewellery and cutting-edge home products.

OUR FAVOURITES: Manuel Tavares p.32. A Arte da Terra p.46. Embaixada p.64.

Eat

You're never far from a restaurant in Lisbon. For diversity, head to the **Bairro Alto** district where you'll find an eclectic array of inexpensive diners alongside ultrahip venues. The **Baixa** caters to Lisbon's workers and has a whole street, Rua das Portas de Santo Antão, largely given over to seafood restaurants. International flavours can be sampled by the Tejo at the **Parque das Nações** and the dockside developments at **Santa Apolónia** and **Doca de Santo Amaro**, while fashionistas head to the cool haunts of **Cais do Sodré**. Some of the best dining experiences, however, are in local neighbourhood restaurants highlighted in the Guide.

OUR FAVOURITES: Mercado da Ribeira p.51. Mini Bar p.55. O Barbas – Catedral p.122.

Drink

The most historic cafés are scattered throughout the **Baixa** and **Chiado** districts, where you'll find locals getting their caffeine fixes throughout the day. You can also get beer, wine or food at these places, though many bars only open after dark (see below). Portuguese beers – largely Sagres and Super Bock – are inexpensive and recommended, while local wines are invariably excellent. Worth sampling too are local brandies; the white variety of port, which makes an excellent aperitif; and a powerful cherry brandy called *ginginha* – several bars in the Baixa specialize in the stuff. Finally, don't miss trying a *caipirinha*, a Brazilian cocktail made from distilled sugar cane, sugar and lime juice.

OUR FAVOURITES: Chapitô à Mesa p.48. Park p.68. Portas Largas p.68.

Go out

Lisbon has a pulsating nightlife, with the highest concentration of clubs and bars in the **Bairro Alto**. Many locals prefer the less frenetic vibe of the **Cais do Sodré** district, which has a handful of cool clubs and happening bars; while the city's biggest clubs are to be found near the river, especially *LuxFrágil* near **Santa Apolónia** and the upmarket venues of **Alcântara**. There are various excellent live music venues, with the **Bairro Alto** and **Alfama** famed for their fado houses.

OUR FAVOURITES: LuxFrágil p.49. Pink Street p.56. Hot Clube de Portugal p.101.

Lisbon at a glance

◁ **Sintra** p.108.
With its fairy-tale palaces, the hilltop town
of Sintra is a must-see day-trip from the capital.

Avenida, Parque Eduardo VII and the Gulbenkian p.90.
The grand Avenida da Liberdade leads to the leafy Parque Eduardo VII;
beyond, the Gulbenkian displays an extraordinarily rich collection of
ancient and modern art.

N

◁ **The Lisbon coast** p.118.
In less than an hour you can reach superb beaches
at Estoril, Cascais or south to Caparica, famed for
its surf and miles of sands.

Belém and Ajuda p.82.
Many of Portugal's maritime explorers
set sail from Belém, home to some of the
city's finest monuments and museums.

Doca de Alcâ

| 0 | metres | 500 |
| 0 | yards | 500 |

Rio Tejo

Alcântara and the docks p.76
Lisbon's docks shelter appealing
riverside bars, clubs, restaurant:
and a couple of top museums.

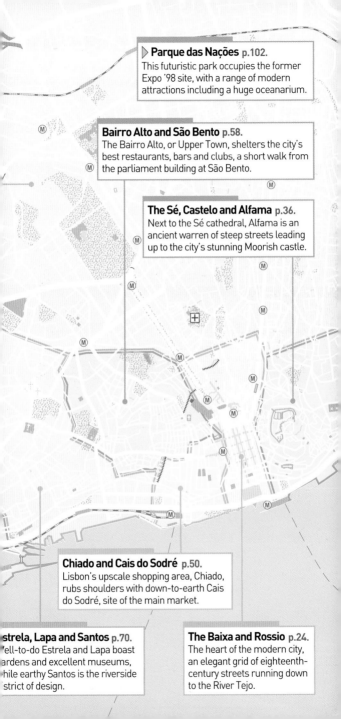

▷ Parque das Nações p.102.
This futuristic park occupies the former Expo '98 site, with a range of modern attractions including a huge oceanarium.

Bairro Alto and São Bento p.58.
The Bairro Alto, or Upper Town, shelters the city's best restaurants, bars and clubs, a short walk from the parliament building at São Bento.

The Sé, Castelo and Alfama p.36.
Next to the Sé cathedral, Alfama is an ancient warren of steep streets leading up to the city's stunning Moorish castle.

Chiado and Cais do Sodré p.50.
Lisbon's upscale shopping area, Chiado, rubs shoulders with down-to-earth Cais do Sodré, site of the main market.

strela, Lapa and Santos p.70.
ell-to-do Estrela and Lapa boast ardens and excellent museums, hile earthy Santos is the riverside strict of design.

The Baixa and Rossio p.24.
The heart of the modern city, an elegant grid of eighteenth-century streets running down to the River Tejo.

15

Things not to miss

It's not possible to see everything that Lisbon has to offer in one trip – and we don't suggest you try. What follows is a selection of the city's highlights, from art-rich museums to melt-in-the-mouth custard tarts.

> Alfama
See page 36
A maze of cobbled streets and tortuous alleys where life continues much as it has for centuries.

< Castelo de São Jorge
See page 40
A former Moorish castle then later a palace and prison, the *castelo* is now one of Lisbon's best viewpoints.

∨ Mosteiro dos Jerónimos
See page 83
Packed with flamboyant Manueline architectural features, this sixteenth-century monastery commemorates Vasco da Gama's discovery of a sea route to India.

< Museu Calouste Gulbenkian
See page 94
Virtually an A–Z of the history of art, from the Mesopotamians to the Impressionists, all set in delightful gardens.

∨ A night out in Bairro Alto
See page 67
The 'high district' is a grid of streets filled with the city's biggest concentration of restaurants, bars and clubs.

< Praça do Comércio
See page 24
The city's grandest square, beautifully arcaded and facing the Tagus, is lined with cafés in classical buildings – the perfect spot for a coffee.

∨ Oceanário
See page 103
This spectacular oceanarium has a massive central tank and is home to all kinds of marine creatures, from sea otters to sharks.

THINGS NOT TO MISS

∧ Mercado da Ribeira (Time Out Market)

See page 51
Part colourful fruit, veg and fish market and part vibrant food hall packed with stalls selling all kinds of dishes and drinks.

< Museu Nacional de Arte Antiga

See page 71
Portugal's national gallery includes works by the likes of Nuno Gonçalves and Hieronymus Bosch.

∧ A ride on a tram
See page 137
The vintage trams are the best way to negotiate Lisbon's steepest gradients and narrow, cobbled streets.

∨ Pink Street
See page 56
This trendy nighttime spot is the place to be seen after dark, filled with hip bars, clubs and fado joints.

∧ Torre de Belém
See page 86
A Lisbon landmark, this iconic ornate tower was built to defend the mouth of the Rio Tejo.

< Pastéis de Belém
See page 89
Head to this famous *pastelaria* for the best custard tarts in town.

<⟨ **A day out in Sintra**

See page 108

A UNESCO World Heritage Site, this attractive wooded hilltop town was the summer retreat for Portuguese royalty whose palaces can still be visited today.

∨ **A day at the beach**

See page 118

It's just a short hop from Lisbon to some excellent Atlantic beaches: those at Cascais and Estoril are easiest to reach.

THINGS NOT TO MISS

Day One in Lisbon

Confeitaria Nacional. See page 34. Start the day with a punchy *bica* coffee in one of Lisbon's most historic cafés, where the decor is as alluring as the pastries.

The Baixa. See page 27. Head down main Rua da Augusta and explore the lively streets and cafés of the Baixa grid.

Chiado. See page 50. Stroll up Rua do Carmo and Rua Garrett where many of Lisbon's best shops can be found.

Lunch. See page 56. Refuel at *Leitaria Académica*, with a simple menu and a smattering of tables outside a lovely square.

Armazéns do Chiado shopping centre

Tram #28. See page 42. This is Lisbon's most famous tram route, grinding back through the Baixa and up towards the Castelo through the Alfama.

Castelo de São Jorge. See page 40. Walk up the steep alleyways to the ruined Moorish castle, the heart of historic Lisbon.

Alfama. See page 43. Tackle the calf-shredding steps to reach the Alfama, Lisbon's village within a city where traditional life still holds sway.

Museu do Fado. See page 44. Gain an insight into the rich history and haunting sounds of Portugal's most distinctive music at this informative museum.

Tram #28

Dinner. See page 49. Try one of the Alfama's fado houses, where you can dine while listening to live music; *A Baiuca* is a good place to start.

Drinks. See page 49. End the night with drinks by the riverside at *LuxFrágil*, one of Europe's coolest clubs.

Museu do Fado

Day Two in Lisbon

Museu Calouste Gulbenkian. See page 94. Take the metro to this superb museum displaying arts and crafts from the time of the Ancient Egyptians right through to the French Impressionists.

Parque Eduardo VII. See page 96. It's a short walk from the museums to Lisbon's main central park famed for its *estufas* – hothouses filled with exotic plants. Be sure to swing by the park's viewing platform for sweeping views of the city.

Praça do Comércio. See page 24. Take the metro or bus to Lisbon's graceful riverside square and follow the waterfront path west for ten minutes until you reach Cais do Sodré.

Museu Calouste Gulbenkian

Lunch. See page 51. Have lunch at one of the many street food stalls in the Mercado da Ribeira, the city's main market.

Mosteiro dos Jerónimos. See page 83. Take the tram to Belém's fantastic monastery, built to give thanks to the success of Portugal's great navigators.

Berardo Collection. See page 85. Don't miss this unbeatable collection of contemporary art, featuring the likes of Andy Warhol and Paula Rego.

Torre de Belém. See page 86. Climb the elaborate sixteenth-century riverside tower that has become the symbol of the city for views of Belém and the river.

Estufas at Parque Eduardo VII

Dinner. See page 64. Make a beeline for *Cervejaria Trindade*, a cavernous beer hall serving great seafood.

Drinks. See page 67. Stick around the Bairro Alto and wait for the nightlife to crank up at its hundreds of little bars and clubs.

Bairro Alto nightlife

Lisbon viewpoints

Built on seven hills, Lisbon has some fantastic *miradouros*, or viewpoints, each with its own distinctive outlook over the skyline – here are the city's most dramatic vantage points.

Miradouro de Santa Luzia. See page 40. The best place to see over the terracotta rooftops and pastel facades of the Alfama and the eastern riverfront.

São Vicente de Fora. See page 42. Climb to the top of this historic church for dizzying views over the eastern corner of Lisbon from its extensive roof.

Castelo de São Jorge. See page 40. Not quite Lisbon's highest hill, but if you clamber around the old ramparts, you'll be able to see all sides of the city.

Parque Eduardo VII. See page 96. The top of the park offers an exhilarating panorama encompassing Lisbon and beyond.

🍴 **Lunch.** See page 101. Chill out by a lake at *Linha d'Água*, which serves good-value buffet lunches at the top of the park.

Miradouro da Graça. See page 42. Superb views over the Castelo and the city beyond can be had from this breezy terrace by the church of Graça.

Miradouro de São Pedro de Alcântara. See page 58. A broad, tree-lined viewpoint from where you can gaze down on the Baixa and the castle opposite.

Miradouro de Santa Catarina. See page 62. Tucked-away *miradouro* with sweeping vistas over the Tejo, a popular hangout for Lisbon's alternative crowd.

🍴 **Dinner.** See page 67. *Noobai* is hidden under the lip of Miradouro de Santa Catarina and serves an array of inexpensive food and drinks.

Cityscape from Miradouro de Santa Luzia

View from São Vicente de Fora

Linha d'Água

Lisbon for families

Lisbon is very family-friendly and children are welcomed everywhere. Below are some of the best attractions for those with kids of any age.

Street lifts. See page 29. There are several wacky street lifts up Lisbon's steepest hills; Elevador de Santa Justa offers great city views.

Oceanário. See page 103. One of the largest in Europe, this stunning building has sharks, rays, otters, penguins and fish galore.

Pavilhão do Conhecimento. See page 102. This interesting science museum has fantastic hands-on experiments and challenges for people of all ages, together with informative exhibits.

Elevador de Santa Justa

🍴 **Lunch.** See page 107. The traffic-free restaurants of Parque das Nações are great for kids – one of the best places for an inexpensive lunch is *Azul Profundo*.

Museu da Marioneta. See page 72. From medieval marionettes to satirical puppets, this museum trumpets an art form that satisfied kids long before computer games.

Museu da Carris. See page 78. Lisbon's trams are great fun to ride on, but here kids can clamber about trams, buses and metro trains with fewer crowds.

Museu da Marioneta

Caparica. See page 121. Lisbon's best beaches are just south of the city, great at any time of the year for a walk or day by the sea.

Sintra. See page 108. Horse and carriage rides, castles and fantasy palaces make this a great day out for any family.

🍴 **Dinner.** See page 33. With lots of space, early-opening *Bonjardim* has tables inside and out, affordable food that kids love, and waiters who are usually extremely child-friendly.

Parque das Nações

PLACES

Bronze fountain, Rossio Square

The Baixa and Rossio

The tall, imposing buildings that make up the Baixa (Lower Town, pronounced bye-sha) house some of Lisbon's most interesting shops. With around 40 hotels and guesthouses, this is also the tourist epicentre, whose needs are served by a range of cafés, restaurants and street entertainers. Facing the river, this area felt the full force of the 1755 earthquake that destroyed much of what was then one of Europe's wealthiest capitals. The king's minister, the Marquês de Pombal, swiftly redesigned the sector with the grid pattern evident today, framed by a triangle of broad squares. Praça do Comércio sits to the south, with Praça da Figueira and Rossio to the north, the latter having been the city's main square since medieval times.

Praça do Comércio

MAP P.26, POCKET MAP E13

The beautiful, arcaded **Praça do Comércio** represents the climax of Pombal's design. Its classical buildings were once a royal palace and the square is centred on an exuberant bronze equestrian statue of Dom José, monarch during the earthquake and the period of the capital's rebuilding. Two of Portugal's last royals came to a sticky end in this square: in 1908 King Carlos I and his eldest son were shot dead here, clearing the way for the declaration of the Republic two years later.

The square has been partly pedestrianized in recent years in a successful attempt to make it more tourist-friendly, with a panoply of cafés and shops on either side. The secluded Patio da Galé, tucked into the western arcades, hosts frequent events, while the Torreão Poente, at the southwest corner of the square, is part of the Museu de Lisboa and hosts temporary exhibits – see Ⓦwww. museudelisboa.pt. The north side of the square is where you can start tram tours of the city. However, it is the square's riverfront that is perhaps most appealing, especially in the hour or two before sunset, when people linger in the golden light to watch the orange ferries ply between the Estação Fluvial ferry station and Barreiro on the other side of the Tejo. An attractive walk is to head west along the pedestrianized riverfront to Cais do Sodré (see page 50).

Praça do Comércio

Rua Augusta

Lisbon Story Centre

MAP P.26, POCKET MAP E13
Praço do Comércio 78–81 Ⓜ Terreiro de Paço ☎ 211 941 027, Ⓦ lisboastorycentre. pt. Daily 10am–8pm. €7; joint ticket with Arco da Rua Augusta €10.

This is the highlight of a group of touristy cafés and shops that fill the square's historic eastern arcades. The **Lisbon Story Centre** gives a potted, visual account of the city's history – good for a rainy day, though somewhat pricey. There are six zones, each dedicated to a phase in Lisbon's past. The multimedia displays include models, paintings, photos, narrations and filmed re-enactments – the highlight is a somewhat gory 4D film depicting the 1755 earthquake, and a "virtual" scale model of the modern city.

Arco da Rua Augusta

MAP P.26, POCKET MAP E13
Ⓜ Terreiro de Paço Ⓦ visitlisboa.com. Mid-April to mid-May, Sept & Oct 9am–8pm; mid-May to Aug 9am–9pm; Nov to mid-April 9am–7pm. €3; joint ticket with Lisbon Story Centre €10.

Praça do Comércio's most prominent building is a huge arch, the **Arco da Rua Augusta**, adorned with statues of historical figures, including the Marquês de Pombal and Vasco da Gama. Acting as a gateway to the city, the arch was built to celebrate Lisbon's reconstruction after the earthquake, although it wasn't completed until 1873. You can take a lift up the structure to just below the Clock Room, a small exhibition space centred round the workings of a nineteenth-century clock. From here, you can squeeze up a spiral staircase to the flat roof of the monument where you'll be greeted by unmissable views across the Praça do Comércio and the Baixa. Don't be tempted to stand under the bell here. When it strikes, you'll regret it.

Rua Augusta

MAP P.26, POCKET MAP D11
Completely paved in mosaics, the broad **Rua Augusta** runs from Praça do Comércio up to Rossio and is the Baixa's main pedestrianized thoroughfare. Filled with shops, market stalls and touristy restaurants, it can get pretty packed, but its buskers and street performers are always entertaining.

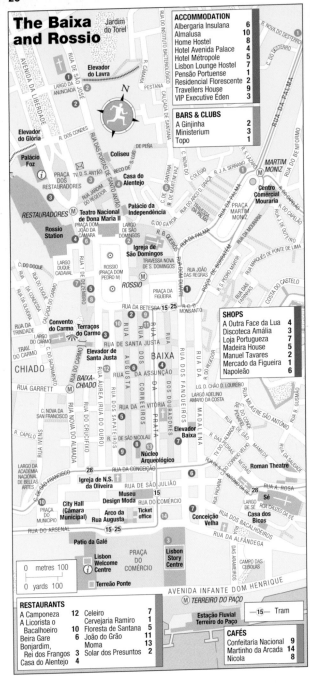

The Baixa and Rossio

ACCOMMODATION

Albergaria Insulana	6
Almalusa	10
Home Hostel	8
Hotel Avenida Palace	4
Hotel Métropole	5
Lisbon Lounge Hostel	7
Pensão Portuense	1
Residencial Florescente	9
Travellers House	2
VIP Executive Éden	3

BARS & CLUBS

A Ginjinha	2
Ministerium	3
Topo	1

SHOPS

A Outra Face da Lua	4
Discoteca Amália	3
Loja Portugueza	7
Madeira House	5
Manuel Tavares	2
Mercado da Figueira	1
Napoleão	6

RESTAURANTS

A Camponesa	12	Celeiro	7
A Licorista o		Cervejaria Ramiro	1
Bacalhoeiro	10	Floresta de Santana	5
Beira Gare	6	João do Grão	11
Bonjardim,		Moma	13
Rei dos Frangos	3	Solar dos Presuntos	2
Casa do Alentejo	4		

CAFÉS

Confeitaria Nacional	9
Martinho da Arcada	14
Nicola	8

15 — Tram

Museu Design Moda

MAP P.26, POCKET MAP E13

Rua Augusta 24 ☎ 218 886 117,
ⓦ mude.pt. Tues–Sun 10am–6pm. Free.

Housed in a grand former bank,
the **Museu Design Moda** is an
impressive collection of design
and fashion classics from the
1930s to today amassed by former
stockbroker and media mogul
Francisco Capelo. The museum's
ever-changing exhibitions include
design classics, such as furniture by
Charles and Ray Eames and Phillipe
Starck, and also features Capelo's
fashion collection – haute couture
from the 1950s, 1960s street
fashion and the brand labelling of
the 1990s. Look out for Ron Arad's
"Big Easy" steel chair (1951), Frank
Gehry's wiggle chair (1972) and
the 1959 Vespa, while fashionistas
will adore Paco Rabanne's metalized
leather boots, Pierre Cardin's 1950s
coats and Alexander McQueen's
superb fur skirt.

Praça do Município

MAP P.26, POCKET MAP D13

The mosaic-paved **Praça do
Município** houses the Neoclassical
nineteenth-century Câmara
Municipal (City Hall), where the
Portuguese Republic was declared
in 1910, flatteringly described by
Portugal's greatest twentieth-century
poet as "one of the finest buildings

Martinho da Arcada

in the city". The square adjoins Rua
do Arsenal, an atmospheric street
lined with pungent shops selling
dried cod, and grocers selling cheap
wines, port and brandy.

The Baixa Grid

MAP P.26, POCKET MAP D11–12

Pombal designed **the Baixa** to have
three main streets dissected by nine
smaller streets. Many of these streets
took their names from the crafts
and businesses carried out there,
like Rua da Prata (Silversmiths'

Fernando Pessoa

Martinho da Arcada, the café at the north end of Praça do
Comércio, was the favoured haunt of Fernando Pessoa (1888–
1935), Portugal's greatest contemporary poet and a leading
figure of twentieth-century modernism. Born in Lisbon, Pessoa
grew up in South Africa before returning to Portugal in 1905
to work as a translator. He spent much of his time composing
poems in Lisbon's cafés. Many of his works are about identity –
he wrote under various alter-egos or "heteronyms", each with
their own personality and style. The most famous are Alberto
Caeiro, Ricardo Reis and Alvaro de Campos, though his most
famous work is the *Book of Disquiet* written under the heteronym
Bernardo Soares. The partly autobiographical work is full of
extraordinary philosophical ruminations that have established his
reputation as a leading existentialist artist.

Street) and Rua dos Sapateiros (Cobblers' Street). Modern banks and shops have disturbed these divisions somewhat, though plenty of traditional stores remain; the central section of Rua da Conceição, for example, is still lined with shops selling beads and sequins. Some of the most interesting streets to explore are the smaller ones running south to north – Rua dos Correeiros, Rua dos Dourados and Rua dos Sapateiros. Pombal also wanted the grid's churches to blend in with his harmonious design, so much so that they are almost invisible – walk along Rua de São Julião and the facade of the church of Oliveira is barely distinguishable from the offices alongside it, though its tiled interior is delightful.

Núcleo Arqueológico

MAP P.26, POCKET MAP E12
Rua dos Correeiros 21 ☎ 211 131 004, ⓦ ind.millenniumbcp.pt. Advance bookings required. Mon–Sat 10am–noon & 2–5pm. Free.

One of Lisbon's smallest but most fascinating museums lies beneath

Núcleo Arqueológico

the Baixa's streets. The remains of Roman fish-preserving tanks, a fifth-century Christian burial place and Moorish ceramics can all be seen in the tiny **Núcleo Arqueológico**, containing the remains of excavations revealed during building work on the BCP bank. Most exhibits are viewed through glass floors or from cramped walkways under the modern bank during a 60-minute tour (tours leave on the hour and alternate between English and Portuguese). Pombal actually rebuilt most of the Baixa on a riverbed, and you can even see the wooden piles driven into the waterlogged soil to support the buildings, the same device that is used in Venice.

If you're interested in discovering more about Lisbon's underground ruins, ask the museum about early summer visits to the amazing Roman tunnels that lie beneath the Baixa. Access is restricted to the 2000-year-old tunnels, whose purpose remains unclear, because they are usually flooded. As a

The Lisbon earthquake

Early eighteenth-century Lisbon had been one of the most active and important ports in Europe, making the Great Earthquake of 1755 all the more tragic. The quake, which was felt as far away as Jamaica, struck Lisbon at 9.30am on November 1 (All Saints' Day), when most of the city's population was at Mass. Within the space of ten minutes there had been three major tremors and the candles of a hundred church altars had started fires that raged throughout the capital. A vast tidal wave later swept the waterfront and, in all, 40,000 of the 270,000 population died. The destruction of the city shocked the continent and prompted religious debate between philosophers Voltaire and Rousseau. For Portugal, it was a disaster that ended its capital's golden age.

result they are open for just three days a year and attract enormous queues. It's a bizarre sight watching people enter the tunnels, which can only be accessed through a manhole cover between tram tracks on Rua da Conceição.

Elevador de Santa Justa

MAP P.26, POCKET MAP D11

Rua de Santa Justa. Daily: March–Oct 7am–11pm; Nov–Feb 7am–9pm. €5 return.

Raul Mésnier's extraordinary and eccentric **Elevador de Santa Justa** was built in 1902 by a disciple of Eiffel. Its giant lift whisks you 32m up the inside of a latticework metal tower, to deposit you on a platform high above the Baixa. Before taking the upper exit on to the Largo do Carmo, head up the dizzy spiral staircase to the pricey rooftop café with great views over the city.

Rossio

MAP P.26, POCKET MAP C11

Praça Dom Pedro IV (popularly known as **Rossio**) has been the city's main square since medieval times and it remains the hub of commercial Lisbon. Its central space sparkles with Baroque fountains and polished, mosaic-cobbled pavements. During the nineteenth century, Rossio's plethora of cafés attracted Lisbon's painters and writers, though many of the artists' haunts were converted into banks in the 1970s. Nevertheless, the outdoor seats of the square's remaining cafés are perennially popular meeting points for groups of friends. On the northwestern side of the square, there's a horseshoe-shaped entrance to Rossio station, a mock-Manueline complex with the train platforms an escalator ride above the street-level entrances.

Teatro Nacional de Dona Maria II

MAP P.26, POCKET MAP D10

Rossio ☎ 213 250 800, ⊛ tndm.pt.

Rossio's biggest concession to grandeur is the **Teatro Nacional de Dona Maria II** built along its north side in the 1840s, and heavily restored after a fire in 1964. Inside there is a good café. Prior to the earthquake, the Inquisitional Palace stood on this site, in front of which public hangings and autos-da-fé (ritual burnings of heretics) took place.

Igreja de São Domingos

MAP P.26, POCKET MAP D11

Largo de São Domingos ☎ 213 428 275. Daily: 7.30am–7pm.

The **Igreja de São Domingos** stands on the site of the thirteenth-century Convento de São Domingos, where sentences were read out during the Inquisition. The convent was destroyed in the earthquake of 1755, though its

Praça dos Restauradores

Praça dos Restauradores

MAP P.26, POCKET MAP C10

The elongated **Praça dos Restauradores** (Square of the Restorers) takes its name from the renewal of independence from Spain in 1640. To the north of the square, the **Elevador da Glória** offers access to the Bairro Alto (see page 58); south sits the superb Art Deco frontage of the old Eden cinema, now an apartment-hotel. The square is dominated by the pink Palácio de Foz on the western side, which housed the Ministry of Propaganda under the Salazar regime (1932–74) but is now home to the Portuguese Tourist Office (see page 141) and tourist police station. During the week it is sometimes possible to visit the palace's ornate upper floors (enquire at the tourist office).

Rua das Portas de Santo Antão

MAP P.26, POCKET MAP D10

The pedestrianized **Rua das Portas de Santo Antão** is well known for its seafood restaurants. Despite the tourist trappings on this and the adjacent Rua Jardim Regedor (you're likely to get waiters trying to smooth-talk you into their premises), it is worth eating here at least once to sample its seafood. The street is also home to several theatres, and the domed **Coliseu dos Recreios** at #96 (☎ 213 240 580, 🌐 www.coliseulisboa.com), which opened in 1890 as a circus but is now one of Lisbon's main concert venues.

Casa do Alentejo

MAP P.26, POCKET MAP D10
Rua de Santo Antão 58 Ⓜ Terreiro de Paço ☎ 213 405 140, 🌐 casadoalentejo.com.pt. Daily 10am–10pm. Free.
A cultural centre with its own café-bar and restaurant (see page 33), the **Casa do Alentejo** is a sumptuously decorated

portal was reconstructed soon after as part of the current Dominican church. For over a century it was the venue for royal marriages and christenings, though it lost this role after the declaration of the Republic and was then gutted by a fire in the 1950s. Some say the fire purged some unsavoury acts that took place on the spot, such as the massacre of forcibly converted Jews (known as "New Christians") which began here in 1506. It was reopened in 1997 after partial restoration to replace the seats and some statues; however, the rest of the cavernous interior and the scarred pillars remain powerfully atmospheric.

Praça da Figueira

MAP P.26, POCKET MAP D11
Praça da Figueira is a historic square (once the site of Lisbon's main market), though the addition of an underground car park has detracted from its former grandeur. Nevertheless, it is slightly quieter than Rossio, and its cafés offer appealing views of the green slopes of the Castelo de São Jorge.

A starter for ten euros?

At restaurants, don't feel you're being ripped off when you're served an array of starters before you even order your main course, then get a bill for what you've eaten at the end. This is normal practice in Portugal and no waiter will take offence if you politely decline whatever you're offered. Starters can vary from simple bread, butter and olives to prawns, cheeses and cured meats. If you're tempted, it's a good idea to ask the waiter how much each item costs. Check your bill, too, to ensure you've not been charged for anything you declined.

pseudo-Moorish palace, little changed for decades. Originally a seventeenth-century mansion and later a casino, it has been a centre dedicated to culture from the Alentejo district since the 1930s. You can just wander in and look around the beautifully tiled interior – some of the tiles are from the original mansion – but most visitors head upstairs to the dining room or café-bar, with its neighbouring ballroom, an amazing, slightly rundown room hung with chandeliers.

Casa do Alentejo

Elevador do Lavra

MAP P.26, POCKET MAP K5
Largo da Anunciada. Mon–Sat 7.50am–7.55pm, Sun 9am–7.55pm. €3.70 return.

Rua das Portas de Santo Antão ends next to where another of the city's classic *elevadores*, **Elevador do Lavra**, begins its ascent. The funicular opened in 1884 and is Lisbon's oldest and least tourist-frequented *elevador*. At the top a short walk down Travessa do Torel takes you to **Jardim do Torel**, a tiny park offering exhilarating views over the city.

Shops

A Outra Face da Lua

MAP P.26, POCKET MAP E12
Rua da Assunção 22. Mon–Sat
10am–7.30pm, Sun noon–7pm.
This buzzy space specializes in
cool retro fashion – fab vintage
clothes, tin toys and the like;
it also has a great attached café
serving light bites such as burgers
and snacks.

Discoteca Amália

MAP P.26, POCKET MAP D11
Rua Áurea 272. Mon–Sat 9am–7pm.
A small but well-stocked shop
named after famous fado singer
Amália Rodrigues, with a good
collection of traditional Portuguese
fado music. If you're looking for
a recommendation, the English-
speaking staff are usually happy to
share their top picks.

Loja Portugueza

MAP P.26, POCKET MAP E13
Rua da Fanquerios 32. Daily 10am–7pm.
A packed treasure-trove of
Portuguese crafts and souvenirs,
including tasteful mugs, tiles, port
and trinkets.

Madeira House

MAP P.26, POCKET MAP D12
Rua Augusta 133. Mon–Sat 9.30am–
7.30pm.
As you'd expect, linens and
embroidery from Madeira feature
heavily here, along with a selection
of attractive ceramics, patterned
tiles and some souvenirs from
the mainland.

Manuel Tavares

MAP P.26, POCKET MAP D11
Rua da Betesga 1a. Mon–Sat 9.30am–
7.30pm.
Small shop dating from 1860,
with a great selection of nuts,
chocolate and national cheeses, and
a basement stuffed with vintage
wines and ports, some dating from
the early 1900s.

Mercado da Figueira

MAP P.26, POCKET MAP E11
Praça da Figueira 10b. Mon–Sat
8.30am–8pm.
The decorative, narrow entrance
hall gives onto a well-stocked
supermarket with a good array of
inexpensive wines, ports and fresh
produce, plus its own café.

Napoleão

MAP P.26, POCKET MAP E12
Rua dos Fanqueiros 68–70. Mon–Sat
9.30am–8pm, Sun 3–7pm.
This spruce shop offers a great
range of quality port and wine from
all Portugal's main regions, and its
enthusiastic, English-speaking staff
can advise on what to buy.

Restaurants

A Camponeza

MAP P.26, POCKET MAP D12
Rua dos Sapateiros 155–157. Mon & Wed–
Sun 7–11pm.
Formerly a *leitaria* (dairy shop) and
still displaying the Art Nouveau
decor from its past existence,
this is now a simple restaurant,
with a short, moderately priced
menu (mains from €9) – the
meat *espetadas* (skewers) are
particularly good.

A Licorista o Bacalhoeiro

MAP P.26, POCKET MAP D11
Rua dos Sapateiros 222–224 ☏ 213 431
415. Mon–Sat noon–3pm & 7–10pm.
This pleasant tile-and-brick
restaurant is a popular lunchtime
stop, when locals flock in for
inexpensive set meals or mains
from around €9.

Beira Gare

MAP P.26, POCKET MAP D11
Praça D. João de Câmara 4. Daily
9am–10pm.
Well-established café-restaurant
situated opposite Rossio station,
serving a menu of stand-up
Portuguese snacks and bargain
meals (mains cost from €7).

Casa do Alentejo

Constantly busy, which is recommendation enough.

Bonjardim, Rei dos Frangos

MAP P.26, POCKET MAP C10

Trav de Santo Antão 11–18 ☎ 213 424 389. Daily noon–11pm (closed Wed all day and Thurs lunch from Oct–March).

A bit of a Lisbon institution thanks to its spit-roast chicken and now so popular that it has spread into three buildings on either side of a pedestrianized alley. There are plenty of tables outdoors, too. A half-chicken is yours for around €9, though it also serves other meat and fish plates at less generous prices.

Casa do Alentejo

MAP P.26, POCKET MAP D10

☎ 213 405 140, ⓦ casadoalentejo.com.pt. Daily noon–3pm & 7–10.30pm.

A centre dedicated to Alentejan culture (see page 30), with its own restaurant, in a beautifully tiled upstairs dining room. Alentejo specialities include oven-roasted rabbit and *carne de porco à alentejana* (grilled pork

with clams), with mains from €11; or just pop in for a drink in the superb bar or courtyard taverna.

Celeiro

MAP P.26, POCKET MAP D11

Rua 1° de Dezembro 65 ☎ 210 306 030, ⓦ celeiro.pt. Mon–Fri 8.30am–8pm, Sat 9.30am–7pm, Sun 9.30–6.30pm.

Located just off Rossio, this inexpensive self-service restaurant sits in the basement of a health-food supermarket and offers tasty vegetarian spring rolls, quiches, pizza and the like from around €6. There's also a streetside café offering a range of snacks and drinks.

Cervejaria Ramiro

MAP P.26, POCKET MAP K5

Avenida Almirante Reis 1 ☎ 218 851 024, ⓦ cervejariaramiro.pt. Tues–Sun noon–12.30am.

Fabulous and famous fish restaurant whose decor has changed little since it opened in 1956. It's spread across three floors; the basement is full of bubbling fish tanks, while the ground floor is usually rammed with clients downing its famed garlic prawns, lobster, crab, *pregos* (steak sandwiches) and the like. The top floors are usually slightly quieter. Turn up early to avoid a wait.

Floresta de Santana

MAP P.26, POCKET MAP D10
Calçada Santana 18 ☏ 963 945 338.
Mon–Sat 10am–10pm.

A short (uphill) walk from the bustle of the Baixa but a world away in terms of atmosphere: excellent-value meals served in a friendly, family-run place which gets busy at lunchtimes. The fish and meat are fresh and generous and desserts are home-made and huge. Two courses with wine come to around €10–15.

João do Grão

MAP P.26, POCKET MAP D11
Rua dos Correeiros 222–226 ☏ 213 424 757. Daily noon–10pm, closed from 3.30–6pm on Mondays and from Oct–March.

One of the better options of the generally disappointing and touristy restaurants on this pedestrianized street, where outdoor tables tempt you to sample the reasonably priced salads, fish and various *bacalhau* dishes (from around €10). The

marble- and azulejo-clas interior is just as attractive.

Moma

MAP P.26, POCKET MAP E12
Rua dos Correeiros 24 ☏ 911 762 349.
Mon–Fri noon–midnight.

Restaurants in the Baixa can be a disappointment but this is an exception, with reliably good-value fish and meat dishes from around €15. Pick between dining in a pleasant and airy space tucked beneath arches, with chequered floor tiles and hanging pendant lights, and a handful of outdoor tables.

Solar dos Presuntos

MAP P.26, POCKET MAP J5
Rua das Portas de Santo Antão 150 ☏ 213 424 253. Mon–Sat 12.30–3.30pm & 7–11.30pm.

The "Manor House of Hams" is, not surprisingly, best known for its smoked ham from the Minho region in northern Portugal, served cold as a starter. There are also excellent, if expensive, meat and seafood dishes, many using traditional recipes. Popular with celebrities; it's best to book a table.

Confeitaria Nacional

Cafés

Confeitaria Nacional

MAP P.26, POCKET MAP D11

Praça da Figueira 18. Daily 8am–8pm.
Opened in 1829 and little changed
since, with a stand-up counter
selling pastries and sweets below
mirrors and stucco ceilings.
There's a little side room as well
as outdoor seating for sit-down
coffees and snacks.

Martinho da Arcada

MAP P.26, POCKET MAP E13

Praça do Comércio 3. Mon–Sat 7am–11pm.
One of Lisbon's oldest café-
restaurants, first opened in 1782 and
declared a national monument in
1910. It has been a gambling den, a
meeting place for political dissidents
and, later, a more reputable hangout
for politicians, writers and artists.
It is now divided into a simple
stand-up café and a slightly pricey
restaurant. The outdoor tables under
the arches are a perfect spot for a
coffee and a *pastel de nata*.

Nicola

MAP P.26, POCKET MAP D11

Rossio 24–25. Daily 8am–midnight.
The only surviving Rossio coffee
house from the early twentieth
century, once the haunt of some
of Lisbon's great literary figures.
The outdoor tables overlooking the
bustle of Rossio are the best feature,
though it has sacrificed much of
its period interior in the name
of modernization. Also has live
fado from Thursday to Saturday
at 8.30pm.

Bars

A Ginjinha

MAP P.26, POCKET MAP D11

Largo de São Domingos 8. Daily
9am–10pm.
Everyone should try *ginginha* –
Portuguese cherry brandy – once.
There's just about room in this

Nicola

microscopic joint to walk in, down
a glassful and stagger outside to see
the city in a new light.

Ministerium

MAP P.26, POCKET MAP E13

Ala Nascente 72, Praça do Comércio ☏ 218
888 454, ⓦ ministerium.pt. Sat 11pm–6am.
The grand and historic buildings
of the former Ministry of Finance
partly make up the stylish
backdrop to this hip club mostly
playing house and techno and
attracting top-name DJs. There's
a spacious dancefloor plus quieter
zones and a great rooftop café-bar
– check the website for details of
events and parties.

Topo

MAP P.26, POCKET MAP E10

Sixth floor, Centro Comercial Martim
Moniz, Praça Martim Moniz ☏ 215 881 322,
ⓦ topo-lisboa.pt. Daily 12.30pm–midnight.
Set on the top floor of a shopping
centre, this contemporary bar-
restaurant has great views towards
the castle from both the light and
airy interior and its outdoor terrace.
The drinks list is as long as the bar,
and it also serves light snacks (from
€6) or pricier mains. At weekends
there are often DJs.

The Sé, Castelo and Alfama

East of the Baixa, the streets climb past the city's ancient cathedral, or Sé, to the dramatic remains of the Castelo de São Jorge, an oasis of tranquillity high above the city. East of the castle lie two of Lisbon's most prominent churches, São Vicente de Fora and Santa Engrácia. The districts around the castle – Mouraria, Santa Cruz and particularly the Alfama – represent the oldest and most atmospheric parts of Lisbon. Down on the riverfront, Santa Apolónia, the international train station, is situated in a revitalized area that boasts the glitzy *LuxFrágil* club and cruise ship terminal, while a little further east lies a historic steam pumping station and a fascinating tile museum.

The Sé

MAP P.38, POCKET MAP F12
Largo da Sé ⓣ 218 876 628. Daily 9am–7pm. Free. Tram #28.

Lisbon's main cathedral, **the Sé**, was founded in 1150 to commemorate the city's Reconquest from the Moors on the site of their main mosque. It's a Romanesque structure with a suitably fortress-like appearance. The great rose window and twin towers form a simple and effective facade, although there's nothing particularly exciting inside: the building was once splendidly embellished on the orders of Dom João V, but his Rococo whims were swept away by the 1755 earthquake and subsequent restorers. All that remains is a group of Gothic tombs behind the high altar and the decaying thirteenth-century **cloister** (daily 10am–7pm; Oct–April closes 6pm; €2.50). This has been heavily excavated, revealing the remains of a sixth-century Roman house and Moorish public buildings.

The Baroque **Treasury** (Mon–Sat 10am–5pm; €2.50) holds a small museum of treasures including the relics of St Vincent, brought to Lisbon in 1173 in a boat that was piloted by ravens, according to legend. Ravens were kept in the cloisters for centuries afterwards, but the tradition halted when the last one died in 1978. To this day, the birds remain one of the city's symbols.

Igreja de Santo António and Museu Antoniano

MAP P.38, POCKET MAP E12
Largo S. António da Sé 22 ⓣ 218 860 447. Tram #28.

The small eighteenth-century church of **Santo António** (open daily) is said to have been built on the spot where the city's most popular saint was born as Fernando Bulhões; after his death in Italy in 1231 he became known as St Anthony of Padua. The tiny neighbouring **museum** (Tues–Sun 10am–6pm; €3, free on Sun mornings) chronicles the saint's life, including his enviable skill at fixing marriages, though only devotees will find interest in the statues and endless images.

Casa dos Bicos

MAP P.38, POCKET MAP F13
Rua dos Bacalhoeiros 10 ⓣ 218 802 040, ⓦ josesaramago.org. Mon–Sat 10am–6pm. €3 (archeological area free).

The **Casa dos Bicos** means the "House of Points", and its curious walls – set with diamond-shaped stones – give an idea of the richness of pre-1755 Lisbon. It was built in 1523 for the son of the Viceroy of India, though only the lower facade of the original building survived the earthquake. It is now owned by the Saramago organization which uses the venue for recitals and a permanent exhibition dedicated to the Nobel Prize in Literature winner and Portuguese author José Saramago, who died in 2010.

The ground floor has been maintained as an archeological area where you can view sections of a third-century Roman wall and fish-processing plant, excavated from beneath the building (Ⓦwww.museudelisboa.pt).

Museu do Aljube – Resistência e Liberdade

MAP P.38, POCKET MAP F12
Rua de Augusta Rosa 42 ☏ 215 818 535, Ⓦ museudoaljube.pt. Tues–Sat 10am–6pm. €3, free Sun 10am–2pm.

This small but engaging and moving **museum** is dedicated to **resistance and freedom**, commemorating those who have been censored or repressed, in particular people who risked their lives during the dictatorship of Salazar (1926–68). Housed in a former political prison, it details the drastic and often brutal lengths Salazar's regime went to hold onto its former colonies and preside over an increasingly weary population up until the 1974 revolution. Exhibits over three floors include old photos and newsreels, radio broadcasts and personal statements from people who were imprisoned here, including Mário Soares (later the Portuguese president) and author Miguel Torga – you can also go inside their former windowless cells, just one by two metres in size.

Museu do Teatro Romano

MAP P.38, POCKET MAP F12
Entrance on Patio de Aljube 5 ☏ 218 820 320, Ⓦ www.museudelisboa.pt. Tues–Sun 10am–1pm & 2–6pm. Free. Tram #28.

The **Museu do Teatro Romano** displays a wealth of Roman coins, spoons and fragments of pots, statues and columns excavated from the ruins of a Roman theatre, dating from 57 AD,

Casa dos Bicos

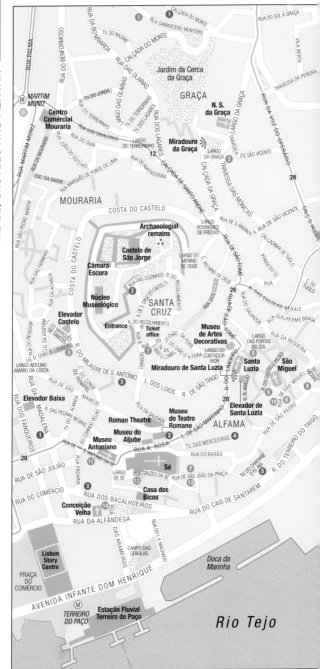

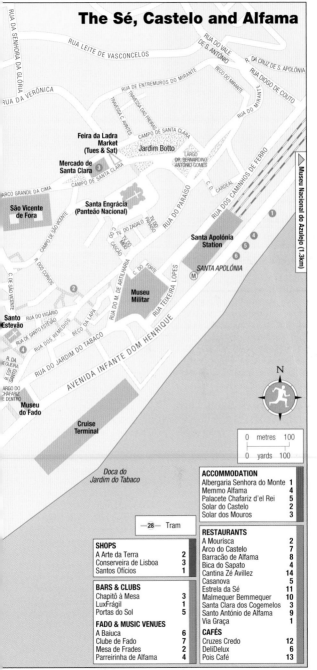

The Sé, Castelo and Alfama

Museu Nacional do Azulejo (1.3km)

RUA DA SENHORA DA GLÓRIA

RUA LEITE DE VASCONCELOS

RUA DA VERÓNICA

RUA DO VALE DE S. ANTÓNIO

R. DA CRUZ DE S. APOLÓNIA

RUA DIOGO DE COUTO

RUA DE ENTREMUROS DO MIRANTE

BECO DO MIRANTE

RUA DO MIRANTE

TRAVESSA DAS PREBAS

TRAVESSA C. AIRES

CAMPO DE SANTA CLARA

Feira da Ladra Market (Tues & Sat)

Jardim Botto

LARGO DR. BERNARDINO ANTÓNIO GOMES

Mercado de Santa Clara 3

CAMPO DE SANTA CLARA

ARCO GRANDE DA CIMA

CARDEAL

RUA DOS CAMINHOS DE FERRO

Santa Engrácia (Panteão Nacional)

RUA DO PARAÍSO

TV. DO ZAGALO

São Vicente de Fora

CAMPO DE SÃO VICENTE

R. DOS CORVOS

C. DE SÃO VICENTE

Santa Apolónia Station

RUA DO FORTE

RUA D. M. DE ARTILHARIA

Santa Apolónia

SANTA APOLÓNIA

Santo Estevão

RUA DO VIGÁRIO

RUA DE SANTO ESTÊVÃO

BECO DA LAPA

RUA DOS REMÉDIOS

RUA TEIXEIRA LOPES

Museu Militar

R. DA REGUEIRA

RUA DO JARDIM DO TABACO

AVENIDA INFANTE DOM HENRIQUE

LARGO DO CHAFARIZ DE DENTRO

Museu do Fado

Cruise Terminal

N

Doca do Jardim do Tabaco

| 0 | metres | 100 |
| 0 | yards | 100 |

28 — Tram

ACCOMMODATION
Albergaria Senhora do Monte	1
Memmo Alfama	4
Palacete Chafariz d'el Rei	5
Solar do Castelo	2
Solar dos Mouros	3

SHOPS
A Arte da Terra	2
Conserveira de Lisboa	3
Santos Ofícios	1

BARS & CLUBS
Chapitô à Mesa	3
LuxFrágil	1
Portas do Sol	5

FADO & MUSIC VENUES
A Baiuca	6
Clube de Fado	7
Mesa de Frades	2
Parreirinha de Alfama	4

RESTAURANTS
A Mourisca	2
Arco do Castelo	7
Barracão de Alfama	8
Bica do Sapato	4
Cantina Zé Avillez	14
Casanova	5
Estrela da Sé	11
Malmequer Bemmequer	10
Santa Clara dos Cogemelos	3
Santo António de Alfama	9
Via Graça	1

CAFÉS
Cruzes Credo	12
DeliDelux	6
Pois Café	13

Museu de Artes Decorativas

which are fenced off just north of Rua Augusto Rosa. Roman Lisbon – Olisipo – became the administrative capital of Lusitania, the western part of Iberia, under Julius Caesar in 60 BC, and the theatre shows the wealth that quickly grew thanks to its fish-preserving industries.

Miradouro de Santa Luzia

MAP P.38, POCKET MAP F12

The church of Santa Luzia marks the entry to the **Miradouro de Santa Luzia**, a spectacular viewpoint where elderly Lisboetas play cards and tourists gather to take in the sweeping views across the Alfama and the river beyond.

Museu de Artes Decorativas

MAP P.38, POCKET MAP F11
Largo das Portas do Sol 2 ⓣ 218 814 600, ⓦ www.fress.pt. Mon & Wed–Sun 10am–5pm. €4. Tram #28 or #12.
Set in the seventeenth-century Azurara Palace, this fascinating **museum** contains some of the best examples of sixteenth- to eighteenth-century applied art in the country. Founded by a

wealthy banker and donated to the nation in 1953, the museum boasts unique pieces of furniture, major collections of gold, silver and porcelain, magnificent paintings and textiles. The rambling building covers five floors, set around a stairway decorated with spectacular *azulejos*. Highlights include a stunning sixteenth-century tapestry depicting a parade of giraffes, beautiful carpets from Arraiolos in the Alentejo district, and oriental-influenced quilts that were all the rage during the seventeenth and eighteenth centuries. The museum also has a small café with a patio garden.

Castelo de São Jorge

MAP P.38, POCKET MAP F11
Bus #37 from Praça da Figueira ⓣ 218 800 620, ⓦ castelodesaojorge.pt. Daily: March–Oct 9am–9pm; Nov–Feb 9am–6pm. €8.50 includes visit to Câmara Escura and Núcleo Museológico.
Reached by a confusing but well-signposted series of twisting roads, the **Castelo de São Jorge** is perhaps the most spectacular building in Lisbon, as much because of its position as anything else. Now Lisbon's most-visited tourist site, the castle was once the heart of a walled city that spread downhill as far as the river. The original Moorish castle on this site was besieged in 1147 by a particularly ruthless gang of Crusaders who, together with King Alfonso I of Portugal, conquered Lisbon after some four hundred years of Moorish rule. Badly damaged during the siege, its fortifications were rebuilt. From the fourteenth century, Portuguese kings took up residence in the old Moorish palace, or Alcáçova, within the walls, but by the early sixteenth century they had moved to the new royal palace on Praça do Comércio. Subsequently, the castle was used as a prison and then as an army barracks until the 1920s. The walls were partly renovated by Salazar

in the 1930s and further restored for Expo '98. A series of gardens, walkways and **viewpoints** hidden within the old Moorish walls makes this an enjoyable place in which to wander about for a couple of hours, with spectacular views over the city from its ramparts and towers.

Câmara Escura

MAP P.38, POCKET MAP F11
Castelo de São Jorge. Weather permitting, daily 10am–5.20pm.

One of the castle towers, the **Tower of Ulysses**, now holds a kind of periscope which projects sights from around the city onto a white disc with commentary in English. Unless you like being holed up in dark chambers with up to fifteen other people, though, you may prefer to see the view in the open air.

Núcleo Museológico and Archeological Remains

MAP P.38, POCKET MAP F11
Castelo de São Jorge. Same hours as castle.

Only a much-restored shell remains of the old Moorish Alcáçova. This now houses the **Núcleo Museológico**, a small museum containing items unearthed during excavations in the castle, including Moorish lamps, Roman storage jars and coins, and pottery and tiles from the seventeenth century. Take time to explore the **Archeological Remains**, an excavation site that includes the scant remains of an Iron Age house, an eleventh-century Moorish quarter and the ruins of the fifteenth-century Palácio dos Condes de Santiago, built for the Bishops of Lisbon.

Santa Cruz and Mouraria

MAP P.38, POCKET MAP F11
Crammed within the castle's outer walls, but free to enter, is the tiny medieval quarter of **Santa Cruz**. This remains a village in its own right, with its own school, bathhouse and church. Leaving Santa Cruz, a tiny arch at the end of Rua do Chão da Feira leads through to Rua dos Cegos and down to Largo Rodrigues de Freitas, which marks the eastern edge of **Mouraria**, the district to which the Moors were relegated after the siege of Lisbon – hence the name. Today Mouraria is an atmospheric residential area.

Mouraria

Miradouro da Graça

MAP P.38, POCKET MAP F10

The **Miradouro da Graça** provides superb views over Lisbon and the castle. To reach it take tram #28 (see page 42) to the broad Largo da Graça. From here, head past Nossa Senhora da Graça – a church which partly dates from 1271, making it one of the oldest in the city – to the viewpoint which also has a small kiosk café-bar. Below the *miradouro*, steps lead down to the Jardim da Cerca da Graça, one of Lisbon's newest parks. There's a children's play area, lawns and appealing walkways.

São Vicente de Fora

MAP P.38, POCKET MAP G11

Largo de São Vicente ☏ 218 810 500. Tues–Sun 10am–6pm. Church free, monastery €5. Tram #28.

The church of **São Vicente de Fora** stands as a reminder of the extent of the sixteenth-century city; its name means "Saint Vincent of the Outside". It was built during the years of Spanish rule by Philip II's Italian architect, Felipe Terzi (1582–1629); its geometric facade was an important Renaissance innovation. Of more interest is the adjoining monastery, home to the world's largest collection of Baroque tiles. Through the beautiful cloisters, decorated with *azulejos* representing scenes from Portugal's history, you can visit the old monastic refectory, which since 1855 has formed the pantheon of the Bragança dynasty. Here, in more or less complete sequence, are the **tombs** of all the Portuguese kings from João IV, who restored the monarchy in 1640, to Manuel II, the last Portuguese monarch who died in exile in England in 1932. Among them is Catherine of Bragança, the widow of England's Charles II, who is credited with introducing the concept of "teatime" to the British. If you have energy, climb to the roof for spectacular views out over the city. There's also a lovely café by the entrance if you do fancy a cup of tea.

Feira da Ladra

MAP P.38, POCKET MAP H10

Campo de Santa Clara. Tues & Sat 9am–around 3pm. Tram #28.

The leafy square of Campo de Santa Clara is home to the twice-weekly **Feira da Ladra** ("Thieves' Market"), Lisbon's main flea market. It's not the world's greatest market, but it does turn up some interesting things, like oddities from the former African colonies and old Portuguese prints. Out-and-out junk – from broken alarm clocks to old postcards – is spread on the ground above Santa Engrácia, with cheap clothes, CDs and half-genuine antiques at the top end of the *feira*. The covered *mercado* (market) building has a fine array of fresh fruit and vegetables.

Tram #28

The picture-book tram #28 (every 15min 5.40am–9.15pm; until 10.30pm on weekends) is one of the city's greatest rides, though its popularity is such that there are usually queues to get on and standing-room-only is more than likely. Built in England in the early twentieth century, the trams are all polished wood and chrome but give a distinctly rough ride up and down Lisbon's steepest streets, at times coming so close to shops that you could almost take a can of sardines off the shelves. From Graça, the tram plunges down through Alfama to the Baixa and up to Prazeres, to the west of the centre. Take care of belongings as pickpockets also enjoy the ride.

Santa Engrácia

Santa Engrácia

MAP P.38, POCKET MAP H10
Campo de Santa Clara ☎ 218 854 820,
🌐 panteaonacional.pt. Tues–Sun: May–Oct
10am–6pm; Nov–April 10am–5pm. €4.
Tram #28.

The white dome of **Santa Engrácia**
makes it the loftiest church
in the city, and it has become
synonymous with unfinished
work – begun in 1682, it was
only completed in 1966. It is now
the **Panteão Nacional**, housing
the tombs of eminent Portuguese
figures, including writer Almeida
Garrett (1799–1854) and Amália
Rodrigues (1920–99), Portugal's
most famous fado singer, and
football legend Eusébio. You can
take the stairs up to the terrace,
from where there are great views
over eastern Lisbon.

The Alfama

MAP P.38, POCKET MAP G12

In Moorish times, the **Alfama**
was the grandest part of the city,
but as Lisbon expanded, the new
Christian nobility moved out,
leaving it to the local fishing
community. None of today's
houses dates from before the
Christian Reconquest, but you'll
notice a kasbah-like layout.
Although an increasing number
of fado restaurants are moving
in, the quarter retains a quiet,
village-like quality. Life continues
much as it has done for years
with people buying groceries and
fish from hole-in-the-wall stores
and householders stoking small
outdoor charcoal grills. Half the
fun of exploring here is getting
lost, but head for Rua de São
Miguel – off which run some of
the most interesting *becos* (alleys)
– and for the parallel street Rua de
São Pedro.

Igreja de Santo Estêvão

MAP P.38. POCKET MAP G11
Largo de Santo Estêvão ☎ 213 912 600.
Open for Sunday Mass only at 10am. Free.
Tram #28.

The handsome church of **Santo
Estêvão** was built in 1733 and
was partly damaged in the 1755
earthquake, leaving it with one of
its two original towers. Its Baroque
interior is impressive but is usually
open only for Mass. However, it's
worth a visit if only to see the view
over the river from its terrace.

Lisbon cruise terminal

Museu do Fado

MAP P.38, POCKET MAP G12

Largo do Chafariz de Dentro 1 ☎ 218 823 470, ⓦ www.museudofado.pt. Tues–Sun 10am–6pm. €5, free on Sun 10am–2pm.
Set in the renovated Recinto da Praia, a former water cistern and bathhouse, the **Museu do Fado** provides a great introduction to this quintessentially Portuguese art form (see box). It also has a good restaurant. The museum details the history of fado and its importance to the Portuguese people; its shop stocks a selection of CDs. A series of rooms contains wax models, photographs, famous paintings of fado scenes and descriptions of the leading singers. It also traces the history of the Portuguese guitar, an essential element of the fado performance. Interactive displays allow you to listen to the different types of fado (Lisbon has its own kind, differing from that of the northern city of Coimbra), varying from mournful to positively racy.

Cruise terminal

MAP P.38, POCKET MAP H12

On most days, an overly large cruise-ship docks at the **cruise terminal** below the Alfama. The terminal is part of an ambitious riverfront redevelopment plan that has cleared away many of the old warehouses, to be replaced by a pedestrianized walkway so that you can stroll along the Tagus all the way from Santa Apolónia train station to Praça do Comércio.

Barbadinhos Steam Pumping Station

POCKET MAP M5

Rua do Alviela 12 ☎ 218 100 215, ⓦ epal.pt. Tues–Sun 10am–5.30pm. €5.
Ten minutes' walk from Santa Apolónia metro, off Calçada dos Barbadinhos, the **Barbadinhos Steam Pumping Station** is a small but engaging museum housed in an attractive old pumping station filled with shiny brass, polished wood and Victorian ingenuity. It was built in 1880 to pump water from a nearby river up Lisbon's steep hills, depositing it in a reservoir hollowed out from a former Franciscan convent. It used four steam-powered engines that worked nonstop until 1928 and which you can see demonstrated today. The museum is the main

Fado

Fado (literally "fate") is often described as a kind of Portuguese blues. Popular themes are love, death, bullfighting and indeed fate itself. It is believed to derive from music that was popular with eighteenth-century immigrants from Portugal's colonies who first settled in Alfama. Famous singers like Maria Severa and Amália Rodrigues grew up in Alfama, which since the 1930s has hosted some of the city's most authentic fado houses – stroll around after 8pm and you'll hear magical sounds emanating from various venues, or better still, enjoy a meal at one of the places listed on page 46. The big contemporary names are Ana Moura and Mariza, who grew up in neighbouring Mouraria. Other singers to look out for (though unlikely to appear in small venues) are Mísia, Carminho, Helder Moutinho, Carlos do Carmo, Maria da Fé, Raquel Tavares, Camané and Cristina Branco.

branch of Lisbon's Museu da Água (water museum; see page 62), and its exhibits give a fascinating insight into the evolution of the city's water supply.

Museu Nacional do Azulejo

MAP P.38, POCKET MAP M5
Rua da Madre de Deus 4. Bus #794 from Praça do Comércio/Santa Apolónia
📞 218 103 340, 🌐 mnazulejo.imc-ip.pt.
Tues–Sun 10am–6pm. €5.

The **Museu Nacional do Azulejo** (tile museum) traces the development of Portuguese *azulejo* tiles from fifteenth-century Moorish styles to the present day, with each room representing a different time period. Diverse styles range from seventeenth-century portraits of the English King Charles II with his Portuguese wife, Catherine of Bragança, to the 1720 satirical panel depicting a man being given an injection in his bottom. The museum is inside the church Madre de Deus, whose eighteenth-century tiled scenes of St Anthony are among the best in the city. Many of the rooms are housed round the church's cloisters – look for the spire in one corner of the main cloister, itself completely covered in tiles. The highlight upstairs is Portugal's longest *azulejo* – a wonderfully detailed 40-metre panorama of Lisbon, completed in around 1738. The museum also has a good café-restaurant and shop.

Patio of the Museu Nacional do Azulejo

Shops

A Arte da Terra

MAP P.38, POCKET MAP F12
Rua de Augusto Rosa 40. Daily 11am–8pm.
Housed in the cathedral's historic
stables – with some of the
handicrafts displayed in the stone
horse troughs – this beautiful space
is filled with local arts and crafts,
from jewellery and cork products to
postcards, preserves and souvenirs.

Conserveira de Lisboa

MAP P.38, POCKET MAP E13
Rua dos Bacalhoeiras 34. Mon–Sat
9am–7pm.
Wall-to-wall tin cans stuffed
into wooden cabinets make this
colourful 1930s shop a bizarre but
intriguing place to stock up on
tinned sardines, squid, salmon,
mussels and just about any other
sea beast you can think of.

Santos Ofícios

MAP P.38, POCKET MAP E12
Rua da Madalena 87. Mon–Sat 10am–8pm.
Small shop crammed with regional
and folk art crafts, including
some attractive ceramics, rugs,
embroidery, baskets and toys.

Restaurants

A Mourisca

MAP P.38, POCKET MAP F10
Largo da Graça 84–85 ☎ 218 863 688.
Tues noon–3pm, Wed–Sun noon–11pm.
Bustling *cervejaria* whose draping
of soccer scarves doesn't quite hide
the beautifully tiled walls. There's
a good range of fish and meat
dishes, including pork steaks and
squid kebabs (€10–11) and *arroz de
marisco* (seafood rice; €25 for two).

Arco do Castelo

MAP P.38, POCKET MAP F12
Rua do Chão da Feira 25 ☎ 218 876 598.
Mon–Sat noon–11pm.
Set just below the entrance to the
castle, specializing in Goan dishes

– there's a fine shrimp curry, and
feijoada indiana (spicy bean stew).
Mains are from €10.

Barracão de Alfama

MAP P.38, POCKET MAP G12
Rua de S. Pedro 16 ☎ 218 866 359.
Tues–Sun 12.30–3pm & 7.30pm–midnight.
An unpretentious *tasca* popular
with locals, with non-touristy
prices: you can have a full meal for
around €20. Portions are generous
with fine fish and grills from €10.

Bica do Sapato

MAP P.38, POCKET MAP M6
Avda Infante Dom Henrique, Armazém
B, Cais da Pedra à Bica do Sapato ☎ 218
810 320, ⓦ bicadosapato.com. Mon 5pm–
midnight, Tues–Sat noon–midnight.
This stylish warehouse conversion
has mirrored walls to reflect the
crisp Tejo vistas. There's an outside
terrace, too. The chef creates what
he calls a "laboratory of Portuguese
ingredients", including black pork
with *migas* (garlic bread sauce) and
tiger prawns as well as roast lamb.
Satisfied guests have included Pedro
Almodóvar, Catherine Deneuve
and architect Frank Gehry, though
its prices (mains €19–26) are about
affordable to mere mortals.

Cantina Zé Avillez

MAP P.38, POCKET MAP E13
Rua dos Arameiros 15 ☎ 215 807 625,
ⓦ cantinazeavillez.pt. Daily noon–
midnight.
Pretty tiled restaurant with tables
outside on the Campo das Cebolas,
serving delicious Portuguese
dishes – try the *pataniscas* (cod
fritters) with black-eyed bean rice,
or octopus with garlic and smoked
paprika (mains from €15).

Casanova

MAP P.38, POCKET MAP M6
Avda Infante Dom Henrique, Loja 7
Armazém B, Cais da Pedra à Bica do Sapato
☎ 218 877 532, ⓦ pizzeriacasanova.pt.
Daily 12.30pm–1.30am.
If *Bica do Sapato* is beyond your
budget, the more modestly priced

Casanova next door offers an array of pizza, pasta and *crostini*, accompanied by similar views from its terrace. It's extremely popular and you can't book, so turn up early. Expect to pay around €15 for a meal and drink.

Estrela da Sé

MAP P.38, POCKET MAP E12
Largo S. António da Sé 4 ☎ 218 870 455.
Mon–Sat 12.30–3pm & 7.30–10pm.
Beautiful *azulejo*-covered restaurant near the Sé, serving inexpensive and tasty dishes like *alheira* (chicken sausage), salmon and Spanish-style tapas from €9. Its wooden booths – perfect for discreet trysts – date from the nineteenth century.

Malmequer Bemmequer

MAP P.38, POCKET MAP G12
Rua de São Miguel 23–25 ☎ 218 876 535.
Wed–Sun 12.30–3.30pm & 7–10pm, Tues 7–10pm.
Cheerily decorated and moderately priced place, overseen by a friendly owner. Grilled meat and fish dishes dominate the menu (try the *salmão no carvão* – charcoal-grilled salmon), or eat from the daily changing tourist menu – mains €11.

Santa Clara dos Cogumelos

MAP P.38, POCKET MAP H10
Mercado de Santa Clara 7 ☎ 218 870 661, ⓦ santaclaradoscogumelos.com. Tues–Sun 7.30pm–11pm, Sat also 1–3pm.
In a lovely room right above the market building, this Italian-run restaurant specializes in mushroom-themed dishes, and very tasty they are, too. Try mushroom risotto, gnocchi, salmon with mushroom sauce, or even porcini-mushroom ice cream. Mains from €14.

Santo António de Alfama

MAP P.38, POCKET MAP G12
Beco de São Miguel 7 ☎ 218 881 328, ⓦ siteantonio.com. Daily 12.30pm–2am.
With a lovely outdoor terrace shaded by trailing vines and

Santa Clara dos Cogumelos

walls covered in black-and-white photos, this restaurant-bar has seating spread across three floors and serves local dishes with an international twist. There's a long list of expensive wines too. Pasta and fish dishes cost from €13, plus there's a range of tapas plates from €7.

Via Graça

MAP P.38, POCKET MAP K5
Rua Damasceno Monteiro 9b ☎ 218 870 830, ⓦ restauranteviagraca.com. Mon–Fri 12.30–3pm & 7.30–11pm, Sat & Sun 7.30–11pm.
Located near the Miradouro da Graça, this sophisticated and highly rated restaurant in an unattractive modern building is better on the inside, from where you can soak up the stunning panoramas across Lisbon. Specialities here include the likes of roast goat, game and *bacalhau*. Dishes cost from around €22 to 30.

Cafés

Cruzes Credo

MAP P.38, POCKET MAP F12

Rua Cruzes da Sé 29 ☎ 218 822 296.
Daily noon–midnight.

This fashionable little café has
a jazzy ambience and serves
tasty *petiscos* snacks, including
bruschetta, hummus and burgers
(€7–8).

DeliDelux

MAP P.38, POCKET MAP M6

Avda Infante Dom Henrique, Armazém B,
Loja 8. Mon–Thurs & Sun 10am–10pm,
Fri & Sat 10am–11pm.

A modern deli with delectable
cheeses, cured meats and preserves,
though the riverside café at the
back is even more appealing –
unless a cruise ship docks and
blocks the view.

Pois Café

MAP P.38, POCKET MAP F12

Rua São João da Praça 93–95 ☎ 218
862 497. Mon noon–11pm, Tues–Sun
10am–11pm.

With its big comfy sofas and
occasional art exhibitions, this
high arched-ceiling café is a must
visit. There's a friendly, young
crowd, books to dip into, cocktails,
healthy brunches, light meals and
home-made snacks, including a
great *apfelstrudel*.

Bars and clubs

Chapitô à Mesa

MAP P.38, POCKET MAP E12

Costa do Castelo 7 ☎ 218 867 734, ⓦ www.
chapito.org. Restaurant Mon–Fri noon–
midnight, Sat & Sun 7.30–midnight. Bar
Mon–Fri 7pm–2am, Sat & Sun noon–2am.

Multipurpose venue incorporating
a theatre, circus school, restaurant
and tapas bar. The restaurant,
Chapitô à Mesa, can be found in
an upstairs dining room, reached
via a spiral staircase, and serves
a range of menus, with mains
such as black pork with ginger or
mushroom risotto from €16. The
outdoor esplanade commands
terrific views over Alfama and
most people come here to drink
and take in the view; reservations
advised. Check the website
for details of live music, films
and readings.

DeliDelux

LuxFrágil

MAP P.38, POCKET MAP M6
Armazém A, Cais da Pedra a Santa Apolónia
Ⓦ luxfragil.com. Thurs–Sat 11pm–6.30am.
This converted former meat
warehouse has become one
of Europe's most fashionable
spaces, attracting A-list visitors
along the likes of Prince and
Cameron Diaz. Part-owned by
actor John Malkovich, it was the
first place to venture into the
docks opposite Santa Apolónia
station. There's a rooftop terrace
with amazing views, various bars,
projection screens, a frenzied
downstairs dancefloor, and
music from pop and trance to
jazz and dance. The club is also
increasingly on the circuit for
touring bands.

LuxFrágil

Portas do Sol

MAP P.38, POCKET MAP G12
Largo Portas do Sol Ⓣ 218 851 299,
Ⓦ portasdosol.biz. Daily 10am–2am.
As you might guess from
the name, this hip spot is an
obligatory venue for anyone
into sunsets. Hiding under the
lip of the road, it's a chic indoor
space, though most people head
straight for the outside seats on
the giant terrace with grandstand
views over the Alfama. The drinks,
coffees and cocktails are pricey,
but more than worth it. DJs
usually play on Friday and
Saturday evenings.

Fado and music venues

A Baiuca

MAP P.38, POCKET MAP G12
Rua de São Miguel 20 Ⓣ 218 867 284.
Mon & Thurs–Sun 7.30–11pm.
Nightly *fado vadio* ("casual" fado)
is performed in this great little
tiled *tasca*, which serves a decent
menu of fresh fish and succulent
grills; minimum spend is €25.
Reservations advised.

Clube de Fado

MAP P.38, POCKET MAP F12
Rua de São João da Praça 86–94
Ⓣ 218 852 704, Ⓦ clube-de-fado.com.
Daily 8pm–2am.
Intimate and homely fado club
with stone pillars, an old well as
a decorative feature, and a mainly
local clientele. It attracts small-
time performers, up-and-coming
talent and the occasional big
name. Expect to pay €60 or so,
including food.

Mesa de Frades

MAP P.38, POCKET MAP L7.
Rua dos Remédios 139a Ⓣ 917 029 436.
Daily 8pm–2.30am.
Set in a beautiful former chapel
and richly adorned with decorative
tiles, this intimate space was in the
spotlight in 2018 when part-time
Lisbon resident Madonna popped
in for an impromptu singalong.
Less illustrious performers are
usually just as engaging.

Parreirinha de Alfama

MAP P.38, POCKET MAP G12
Beco do Espírito Santo 1 Ⓣ 218 868 209,
Ⓦ parreirinhadealfama.com. Tues–Sun
8pm–1am.
One of the best fado venues owned
by famous fado singer Argentina
Santos, just off Largo do Chafariz
de Dentro, often attracting leading
stars and an enthusiastic local
clientele. Reservations are advised
when the big names appear.

Chiado and Cais do Sodré

The well-to-do district of Chiado (pronounced she-ar-doo) is famed for its smart shops and cafés, along with the city's main museum for contemporary arts. Down on the waterfront, Cais do Sodré (pronounced kaiysh-doo-soodray) is one of the city's "in" districts. Many of its waterfront warehouses have been converted into upmarket cafés and restaurants and by day, in particular, a stroll along its characterful riverfront is very enjoyable. Nearby Mercado da Ribeira, Lisbon's main market, is also big on atmosphere, as is the hillside Bica district, which is served by another of the city's classic funicular street lifts – Elevador da Bica. Cais do Sodré is also where you can catch ferries across the Tejo to the little port of Cacilhas which not only has some great seafood restaurants with views over Lisbon, but is also the bus terminus for some of the region's best beaches and for the spectacular Cristo Rei statue of Christ.

Rua Garrett

MAP P.52, POCKET MAP C12

Chiado's most famous street, **Rua Garrett**, is where you'll find some of the oldest shops and cafés in the city, including *A Brasileira* (see page 56). Beggars usually mark the nearby entrance to the **Igreja dos Mártires** (Church of the Martyrs), named after the English Crusaders who were killed during the siege of Lisbon. Some of the area's best shops can also be found in nearby Rua do Carmo. This was the heart of the area that was greatly damaged by a fire in 1988, although the original *belle époque* atmosphere has since been superbly re-created under the direction of eminent Portuguese architect Álvaro Siza Vieira.

Museu Nacional de Arte Contemporânea do Chiado

MAP P.52, POCKET MAP C13
Rua Serpa Pinto 4 ☎ 213 432 148, ⓦ museuartecontemporanea.gov.pt. Tues–Sun 10am–6pm. €4.50, free Sun 10am–2pm.

The **National Museum of Contemporary Art** traces the history of art from Romanticism to Modernism. It is housed in a stylish building with a pleasant courtyard café and rooftop terrace, constructed around a nineteenth-century biscuit factory. Within the gallery's permanent collection are works by some of Portugal's most influential artists since the nineteenth century, along with foreign artists influenced by Portugal including Rodin. Highlights include Almada Negreiros' 1920s panels from the old São Carlos cinema, showing Felix the Cat; a beautiful sculpture, *A Viúva* (The Widow), by António Teixeira Lopes; and some evocative early twentieth-century Lisbon scenes by watercolourist Carlos Botelho. There are also frequent temporary exhibitions.

Elevador da Bica

MAP P.52, POCKET MAP B13
Entrance on Rua de São Paulo. Mon–Sat 7am–9pm, Sun 9am–9pm. €3.70 return.

With its entrance tucked into an arch on Rua de São Paulo, the **Elevador da Bica** is one

Tram #25 to Prazeres

You can catch another of Lisbon's classic tram rides, the #25, from Praça da Figueira (Mon–Fri every 15min 6.30am–8.30pm). This sees far fewer tourists than tram #28 (see page 42) but takes almost as picturesque a route. From here it trundles along the riverfront and up through Lapa and Estrela to the suburb of Prazeres, best known as the site of one of Lisbon's largest cemeteries. You can stroll round the enormous plot where family tombs are movingly adorned with trinkets and photos of the deceased.

of the city's most atmospheric funicular railways. Built in 1892 – and originally powered by water counterweights, but now electrically operated – the *elevador* leads up towards the Bairro Alto, via a steep residential street. Take time to explore the steep side-streets of the Bica neighbourhood, too, a warren of characterful houses, little shops and fine local restaurants.

Mercado da Ribeira

MAP P.52, POCKET MAP B13
Main entrance on Avda 24 de Julho 📞 212 244 980, 🌐 timeoutmarket.com/lisboa. Fruit, fish and vegetable market Mon–Sat 6am–2pm; food stalls Mon–Wed & Sun 10am–midnight, Thurs–Sat 10am–2am.

Built originally on the site of an old fort at the end of the nineteenth century, the **Mercado da Ribeira** is Lisbon's most historic market, though the current structure dates only from 1930. Inside, stalls sell an impressive array of fresh fish, fruit and vegetables, with a separate, aromatic flower section. However, much of the building is now given over to the vibrant Time Out Market Lisboa, filled with an impressive range of food stalls and plenty of communal benches; it's a great place to sample dishes from some of the city's top chefs, such as Alexandre Silva and Henrique Sá Pessoa, or you can choose something simple like a *prego* (steak sandwich) or pizza.

Mercado da Ribeira

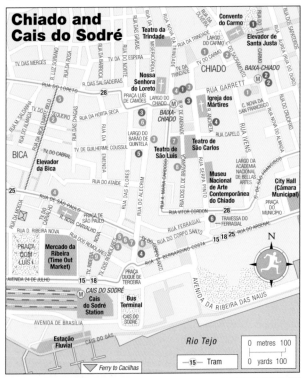

Chiado and Cais do Sodré

ACCOMMODATION	
Hotel Bairro Alto	3
Hotel Borges	1
Hotel do Chiado	2
LX Boutique	4

SHOPS	
Armazéns do Chiado	2
A Vida Portuguesa	4
Fábrica Sant'Anna	5
Livraria Bertrand	3
Luvaria Ulisses	1
Storytailors	6

RESTAURANTS	
Cantinho do Avillez	8
Casa Liège	5
Cervejaria Farol	10
La Brasserie L'Entrecôte	6
Mini Bar	7
Rio Grande	9

CAFÉS	
Café a Brasileira	4
Café Vertigo	1
Leitaria Académica	2
Pastelaria Benard	3

BARS	
Arco da Velha	4
A Tabacaria	9
Bicaense	2
Intermezzo	1
MusicBox	8
Palácio Chiado	3
Pensão Amor	7
Povo	5
Sol e Pesca	6

Travel to Cacilhas and beyond

Cais do Sodré is the main departure point for ferries over the Tejo to the largely industrial suburbs to the south. Ferries to Cacilhas (ⓦwww.transtejo.pt; every 15min, 5.35am–1.40am, last return 1.20am; €1.25 single) dock by a bus and tram depot from where buses run to Costa da Caparica (see page 121).

You pay slightly above the norm for the concept and ambience, but with everything from hams, cheeses and grilled chicken to gourmet burgers, seafood, organic salads and chocolates (not to mention champagne and cocktail bars), you might well find yourself tempted back here again and again. On Sunday mornings there's a collectors' market.

Rua Cor-de-Rosa

POCKET MAP C13

Rua Nova do Carvalho's once dodgy clubs and bars have now (largely) been revamped into some of the city's coolest hangouts. The rebranding has extended to the colour of the street, which is now pink, hence the nickname **Rua Cor-de-Rosa** (Pink Street). We list some of the best places on page 56.

Cacilhas and Almada

MAP P.52, POCKET MAP J8

The short, blustery ferry ride from Lisbon's Cais do Sodré over the Tejo to Cacilhas is great fun and grants wonderful views of the city. **Cacilhas** is little more than a bustling bus and ferry terminal with a pretty church, surrounded by lively stalls and cafés, but is well known for its seafood restaurants. You can also visit the wooden-hulled, fifty-gun **Dom Fernando II e Glória frigate** (ⓣ917 841 149, ⓦccm.marinha.pt; Mon noon–6pm, Tues–Sun 10am–6pm (closes 5pm from Oct–April; €4) on Largo Alfredo Diniz. Built in India in 1843, it's now a museum showing what life at sea was like in the mid-nineteenth century. A good riverside walk is to head west towards the bridge along the waterfront. It's around fifteen minutes' walk to the **Elevador Panorâmico da Boca do Vento** (daily 8am–midnight; €2 return), a sleek lift that whisks you 30m up the cliff face to the attractive old part of **Almada**, giving fantastic views.

Cristo Rei

MAP P.52, POCKET MAP H9
Bus #101 from outside the Cacilhas ferry terminal ⓣ212 751 000, ⓦcristorei.pt. Lift open daily 9.30am–6.30pm. €5 return.
On the heights above Almada stand the outstretched arms of **Cristo Rei** (Christ the King). Inspired by Rio's famous *Cristo Redentor* statue, it was built in 1959 as a pilgrimage site to grace Portugal's non-participation in World War II. A lift shuttles you 80m up the plinth, where a few stairs lead to a dramatic viewing platform at the foot of the statue, from which, on a clear day, you can catch a glimpse of the glistening roof of the Pena palace at Sintra.

Cristo Rei

Shops

A Vida Portuguesa

MAP P.52, POCKET MAP C12
Rua Anchieta 11. Mon–Sat 10am–8pm,
Sun 11am–8pm.

An expensive but evocative collection of retro toys, crafts and ceramics, beautifully displayed and packaged in a former perfumery.

Armazéns do Chiado

MAP P.52, POCKET MAP D12
Rua do Carmo 2. Daily 10am–10pm,
restaurants until 11pm.

This swish shopping centre sits on six floors above metro Baixa-Chiado in a structure that's risen from the ashes of the Chiado fire, though it retains its traditional facade. Shops include Pepe Jeans, Fnac, The Body Shop and Sunglass Hut. The top floor has a series of cafés and restaurants, most with great views.

Fábrica Sant'Anna

MAP P.52, POCKET MAP C13
Rua do Alecrim 95. Ⓦ santanna.com.
Mon–Sat 9.30am–7pm.

A great place to find out more about Portuguese *azulejos*, and

to buy a few souvenirs to take home. Founded in 1741, the factory shop still makes ceramics on the premises using traditional techniques and sells a wide range of handmade ceramics, plus copies of classic designs.

Livraria Bertrand

MAP P.52, POCKET MAP C12
Rua Garrett 73. Mon–Sat 9am–10pm,
Sun 11am–8pm.

Officially the world's oldest bookshop, this charming, cavernous shop was founded in 1732 and was once the meeting place for Lisbon's literary set. Offering novels in English and a range of foreign magazines, it's also a good place to find English translations of Portuguese writers, including the famous poet Fernando Pessoa.

Luvaria Ulisses

MAP P.52, POCKET MAP D11
Rua do Carmo 87a. Mon–Sat 10am–7pm.

The superb, ornately carved wooden doorway leads you into a minuscule glove shop, with hand-wear to suit all tastes tucked into rows of boxes.

Storytailors

Storytailors

MAP P.52, POCKET MAP C13
Calçada do Ferragial 8. Tues–Sat
11am–7pm.

Set in a suitably stylish, bare-brick eighteenth-century former warehouse, the shop interior is as magical as its designer clothes inspired by fairy tales. Its haute couture range has been snapped up by the likes of Madonna and Lily Allen, though you'll need a rock star's salary to afford it.

Restaurants

Cantinho do Avillez

MAP P.52, POCKET MAP C13
Rua dos Duques de Bragança 7
211 992 369, cantinhodoavillez.pt.
Mon–Fri 12.30–3pm & 7pm–midnight,
Sat & Sun 12.30pm–midnight.

In a contemporary space, with tram #28 rattling by its door, this laidback but classy canteen is a good place to sample food from Lisbon's top chef, José Avillez, at reasonable prices. Delectable mains from €18 include the likes of scallops with sweet potatoes and asparagus, or Alentejo pork with coriander. Starters include a superb baked Nisa cheese, and the house wines are equally top-notch.

Casa Liège

MAP P.52, POCKET MAP B12
Rua da Bica Duarte Belo 72–74
213 422 794. Mon–Sat 11am–11pm.

Small and bustling *tasca* at the top end of the Elevador da Bica, packed at lunchtimes thanks to filling and inexpensive dishes such as grilled chicken, sausages and fine *pastéis de bacalhau* (cod fritters) from under €8. Good house wine, too.

Cervejaria Farol

MAP P.52, POCKET MAP H9
Alfredo Dinis Alex 1–3, Cacilhas
212 765 248, restaurantefarol.com.
Daily noon–11pm.

The most high-profile seafood restaurant in Cacilhas, with fine views across the Tejo to match. If you feel extravagant, it's hard to beat the lobster, though other fish dishes are yours from around €12. *Azulejos* on the wall show the old *farol* (lighthouse) that once stood here – the restaurant is located along the quayside, on the right as you leave the ferry.

La Brasserie L'Entrecôte

MAP P.52, POCKET MAP C12
Rua do Alecrim 117–120 213 473 616,
brasserieentrecote.pt. Daily 12.30–3pm
& 7.30–11.30pm.

This upmarket restaurant has won awards for its entrecôte steak which is just as well, as that's all it serves. With a sauce said to contain 35 ingredients, it is truly delicious. Mains from €18–25. Reservations advised.

Mini Bar

MAP P.52, POCKET MAP C12
Rua António Maria Cardoso 58
211 305 393, minibar.pt. Daily
7pm–1am, bar til 2am.

There's certainly a theatrical element to the cuisine in this buzzy restaurant-bar inside the Art Deco Teatro de São Luiz. Various themed tasting menus feature innovative and quirky tapas-style dishes (€3–15), including Algarve prawns, tuna and mackerel ceviche and beef croquettes. Some of top chef José Avillez's creations are decidedly Blumenthal-esque, including amazing 'edible' cocktails and 'exploding' olives. Highly recommended.

Rio Grande

MAP P.52, POCKET MAP B12
Rua Nova do Carvalho 55 213 423 804.
Mon, Tues & Thurs–Sun 12.30pm–3pm &
6–11pm.

It might be on a street full of hip bars, but Rio Grande is reassuringly traditional, with *azulejos* on the walls beneath an arched ceiling. The spacious restaurant serves up good-value Portuguese classics such as pork steaks and a good array of fresh fish for under €9.

Cafés

Café a Brasileira

MAP P.52, POCKET MAP C12

Rua Garrett 120. Daily 8am–2am.

Opened in 1905, and marked by an outdoor bronze statue of the poet Fernando Pessoa, this is the most famous of Lisbon's old-style coffee houses. The tables on the pedestrianized street get snapped up by tourists but the real appeal is in its traditional interior, where prices are considerably cheaper, especially if you stand at the long bar. At night buskers often add a frisson as the clientele changes to a more youthful brigade, all on the beer.

Café Vertigo

MAP P.52, POCKET MAP C12

Trav do Carmo 4 ☎ 213 433 112.
Mon–Sat 8am–10pm.

An arty crowd frequents this attractive café with an ornate glass ceiling. Occasional art exhibits and a good range of cakes and organic snacks.

Leitaria Académica

MAP P.52, POCKET MAP C12

Largo do Carmo 1–3. Mon–Sat 7am–11pm,
Sun 7am–8pm.

Outdoor tables on one of the city's leafiest squares. Besides drinks and snacks, it also serves up a menu

Café A Brasileira

of light lunches; the tasty grilled sardines are perfect in summer.

Pastelaria Benard

MAP P.52, POCKET MAP C12

Rua Garrett 104. Mon–Sat 8am–11pm.

Often overlooked because of its proximity to *Café A Brasileira*, this ornate nineteenth-century café offers superb cakes, ice cream and coffees; it also has a popular outdoor terrace on Chiado's most fashionable street.

Bars and clubs

Arco da Velha

MAP P.52, POCKET MAP B13

Rua de Sao Paulo 184–186 ☎ 218 220 843.
Mon–Thurs & Sun 12.30pm–midnight,
Fri 12.30pm–2am, Sat 11.30am–2am.

This quirky space is part antique store and part café-bar, where you can browse around interesting furniture and knick-knacks over a coffee and home-made cake or a glass of wine with *petiscos*.

A Tabacaria

MAP P.52, POCKET MAP B13

Rua de São Paulo 75–77 ☎ 213 420 281.
Daily 6pm–2am.

In a wonderful old tobacco shop dating back to 1885 – with many of the original fittings – this cosy bar specializes in cocktails (from €7), made from gin, vodka, whisky and seasonal fruits.

Bicaense

MAP P.52, POCKET MAP B12

Rua da Bica Duarte Belo 38–42. Tues–Sat
7pm–2am.

Small, fashionable bar on the steep street used by the Elevador da Bica, with occasional live jazz and Latin sounds; good cocktails; and a moderately priced bar-food menu.

Intermezzo

MAP P.52, POCKET MAP D12

Rua Garrett Patio 19. Mon–Sat
12.30pm–11pm.

With a handful of outside seats tucked away in a hidden courtyard,

MusicBox

this stylish little modern bar rustles together a mean range of cocktails and other drinks; its sister *Mezzogiorno* next door also serves decent pizzas.

MusicBox

MAP P.52, POCKET MAP C13
Rua Nova do Carvalho 24 ☎ 213 430 107, ⓦ musicboxlisboa.com. Mon–Sat 11pm–6am.

Tucked under the arches of Rua Nova do Carvalho is this cool cultural and music venue which hosts a mix of club nights, live music, films and performing arts, with a strong emphasis on promoting independent acts. There's a top sound and light system and usually a buzzy, happy crowd.

Palácio Chiado

MAP P.52. POCKET MAP C12
Rua do Alecrim 70 ☎ 212 442 270, ⓦ palaciochiado.pt. Sun–Thurs noon– midnight, Fri & Sat noon–2am.

This ornate former palace has been transformed into a hip outlet for various bars and restaurants. Head to the top floor for a stunning bar area, complete with a golden-winged lion suspended overhead, for a range of tantalising cocktails, including O Mistério, a cherry liqueur with lime and basil. The adjacent room has good views over Chiado.

Pensão Amor

MAP P.52, POCKET MAP C13
Rua do Alecrim 19 ☎ 213 143 399. Daily 2pm–3am.

The "Pension of Love" is a former "house of ill-repute". It has retained its eighteenth-century burlesque fittings for its current incarnation as a trendy bar with risqué photos, frescoes and mirrors. You can browse through the small erotic bookstore or enjoy occasional live concerts.

Povo

MAP P.52, POCKET MAP C13
Rua Nova do Carvalho 32–26 ☎ 213 473 403, ⓦ povolisboa.com. Mon–Wed & Sun 6pm–4am, Thurs–Sat 6pm–2am.

This fashionable tavern offers fado from up-and-coming stars (Tues– Sun from 8pm) and late-night DJs at weekends in the heart of "Pink Street". There's a great menu of *petiscos* and mains such as mussels with seaweed, *bacalhau* dishes and steaks (€8–21).

Sol e Pesca

MAP P.52, POCKET MAP C13
Rua Nova do Carvalho 44 ☎ 213 467 203. Daily noon–2am.

Once a shop selling fishing equipment, this is now a hip bar. The fishing equipment is part of the decor, and you can still purchase tinned fish to enjoy with bread and wine at low stools inside, or outside on trendy "Pink Street".

Bairro Alto and São Bento

The Bairro Alto, the Upper Town, sits on a hill west of the Baixa. After the 1755 earthquake, the relatively unscathed district became the favoured haunt of Lisbon's young bohemians. Home to the Institute of Art and Design and various designer boutiques, it is still the city's most fashionable district. By day, the central grid of narrow, cobbled streets feels residential. After dark, however, the area throngs with people visiting its famed fado houses, bars and restaurants, while the city's LGBTQ community coalesces around the clubs of neighbouring Príncipe Real. There are impressive monuments too, including the Palácio da Assembléia, Portugal's parliamentary building in nearby São Bento. This area houses good ethnic restaurants, a legacy of the city's first black community established by the descendants of African slaves.

Elevador da Glória

MAP P.60, POCKET MAP C11
Mon–Thurs 7am–11.55pm, Fri 7am–12.25am, Sat 8.45am–12.25am, Sun 9.15am–11.55pm. €3.70 return.
Everyone should ride the **Elevador da Glória** at least once. From the bottom of Calçada da Glória

Elevador da Glória

(off Praça dos Restauradores, see page 30), the funicular climbs the knee-jarringly sheer street in a couple of minutes, leaving the lower city behind as you ascend above its rooftops. An amazing feat of engineering, the tram system was built in 1885. It was originally powered by water displacement, later replaced by steam, and now runs on electricity.

At the top, pause at the gardens, the **Miradouro de São Pedro de Alcântara**, from where there's a superb view across the city to the castle.

Igreja de São Roque

MAP P.60, POCKET MAP C11
Largo de Trindade Coelha ☏ 213 235 383, ⓦ www.museu-saoroque.com. April–Sept Mon 2–7pm, Tues–Sun 10am–7pm; Oct–March Mon 2–6pm, Tues–Sun 10am–6pm. Free.
The sixteenth-century **Igreja de São Roque** looks like the plainest church in the city, with its bleak Renaissance facade. Yet inside lies an astonishing succession of lavishly decorated side chapels. The highlight is the **Capela de**

São João Baptista, for its size the most expensive chapel ever constructed. It was ordered from Rome in 1742 by Dom João V to honour his patron saint and, more dubiously, to gratify Pope Benedict XIV whom he had persuaded to confer a patriarchate on Lisbon. It was erected at the Vatican for the Pope to celebrate Mass in, before being dismantled and shipped to Lisbon at the then vast cost of £250,000. If you examine the four "oil paintings" of John the Baptist's life, you'll find that they are in fact intricately worked mosaics. The more valuable parts of the altar front are kept in the adjacent **museum** (same hours as church; €2.50, free Sun 9am–2pm), which also displays sixteenth- to eighteenth-century paintings and a motley collection of church relics.

Convento do Carmo

MAP P.60, POCKET MAP D12
Largo do Carmo ☎ 213 478 629,
🌐 museuarqueologicodocarmo.pt.
Mon–Sat: June–Sept 10am–7pm;
Oct–May 10am–6pm. €4.

Built between 1389 and 1423, and once the largest church in the city, the **Convento do Carmo** was partially destroyed by the 1755 earthquake but is even more striking as a result, with its beautiful Gothic arches rising grandly into the sky. Today it houses the splendid **Museu Arqueológico do Carmo**, home to many of the treasures from monasteries that were dissolved after the 1834 revolution. The entire nave is open to the elements, with columns and statuary scattered in all corners. Inside, on either side of what was the main altar, are the main exhibits, centring on a series of tombs. Largest is the beautifully carved, stone tomb of Ferdinand I; nearby, that of Gonçalo de Sousa, chancellor to Henry the Navigator, is topped by a statue of Gonçalo himself. There is also an Egyptian sarcophagus, whose inhabitant's

Convento do Carmo

feet are just visible underneath the lid; and, equally alarmingly, two pre-Columbian mummies which lie in glass cases, alongside the preserved heads of a couple of Peruvian Indians.

The exit to the **Elevador de Santa Justa** (see page 29) is at the side of the Convento do Carmo – go onto the rampway leading to it for fine views over the city or the partly lawned terrace in front, the **Terraços do Carmo**, with its handy café.

Bairro Alto

MAP P.60, POCKET MAP B11

Quiet by day, the graffitied central streets of the **Bairro Alto** buzz with people after dark, especially on summer weekends when the streets become a giant mass of partygoers. The liveliest area is the tight network of streets to the west of Rua da Misericórdia, particularly after midnight in Rua do Norte, Rua Diário de Notícias, Rua da Atalaia and Rua da Rosa. Running steeply downhill, Rua do Século is one of the area's most historic streets. A sign at no. 89 marks the birthplace of the Marquês de Pombal, the minister responsible for rebuilding Lisbon after the Great Earthquake.

Bairro Alto and São Bento

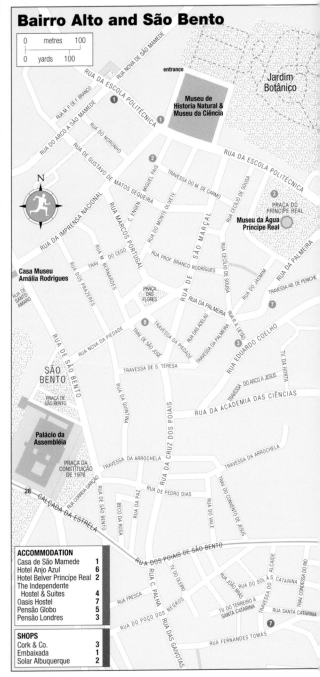

ACCOMMODATION	
Casa de São Mamede	1
Hotel Anjo Azul	6
Hotel Belver Princípe Real	2
The Independente	
Hostel & Suites	4
Oasis Hostel	7
Pensão Globo	5
Pensão Londres	3

SHOPS	
Cork & Co.	3
Embaixada	1
Solar Albuquerque	2

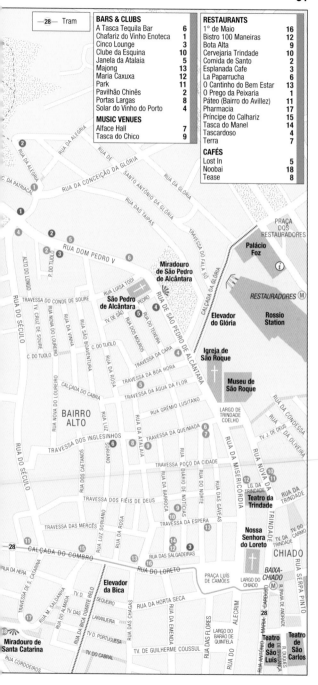

| — 28 — | Tram |

BARS & CLUBS

A Tasca Tequila Bar	6
Chafariz do Vinho Enoteca	1
Cinco Lounge	3
Clube da Esquina	10
Janela da Atalaia	5
Majong	13
Maria Caxuxa	12
Park	11
Pavilhão Chinês	2
Portas Largas	8
Solar do Vinho do Porto	4

MUSIC VENUES

| Alface Hall | 7 |
| Tasca do Chico | 9 |

RESTAURANTS

1° de Maio	16
Bistro 100 Maneiras	12
Bota Alta	9
Cervejaria Trindade	10
Comida de Santo	2
Esplanada Cafe	6
La Paparrucha	6
O Cantinho do Bem Estar	13
O Prego da Peixaria	1
Páteo (Bairro do Avillez)	11
Pharmacia	17
Príncipe do Calhariz	15
Tasca do Manel	14
Tascardoso	4
Terra	7

CAFÉS

Lost In	5
Noobai	18
Tease	8

Miradouro de Santa Catarina

MAP P.60, POCKET MAP A12
Tram #28.

At the bottom end of the Bairro Alto grid, set on the cusp of a hill high above the river, the railed **Miradouro de Santa Catarina** has spectacular views. Here, in the shadow of the statue of the Adamastor – a mythical beast from Luís de Camões's *Lusiads* – a mixture of oddballs and New Age types often collects around an alluring drinks kiosk, built in 1883, (daily 10am–dusk, weather permitting), which has a few outdoor tables.

Praça do Príncipe Real

MAP P.60, POCKET MAP A10
Bus #758 from Chiado.

North of the Bairro Alto, the streets open out around the leafy **Praça do Príncipe Real**, one of the city's loveliest squares. Laid out in 1860 and surrounded by the ornate homes of former aristocrats – now mostly shops or offices – the square is the focal point of Lisbon's LGBTQ scene, though by day it is largely populated by families or locals playing cards under the trees.

Museu da Água Príncipe Real

MAP P.60, POCKET MAP A10
Praça do Príncipe Real 1. Bus #758 from Chiado ☎ 218 100 215, ⓦ bit.ly/ AguaPrincipeReal. Tues–Sat 10am–5.30pm. €3. Tours Sat 11am & 3pm. €3.

The **Museu da Água Príncipe Real** is accessed down steps in the centre of the square of the same name. Inside is an eerie nineteenth-century reservoir, where you can admire brick and vaulted ceilings, part of a network of tunnels that links up with the Aqueduto das Águas Livres (see page 94). Not for claustrophobics, the tours (book in advance) take you along one of these, a humid 410m tunnel that exits at the viewpoint of Miradouro de São Pedro (see page 58).

Museu Nacional de História e da Ciência

MAP P.60, POCKET MAP H5
Rua Escola Politécnica 56. Bus #758 from Chiado ⓦ museus.ulisboa.pt. Tues–Fri 10am–5pm, Sat & Sun 11am–6pm; closed Aug. €5, combined ticket €6, includes entry to Jardim Botânico.

The nineteenth-century Neoclassical former technical college now hosts the mildly engaging museums of natural history known as the Museus de Politécnica. The **Museu da Ciência** (whose labs featured in the film *The Promise*, starring Christian Bale) has some absorbing geological exhibits and a low-tech interactive section where you can balance balls on jets of air and swing pendulums among throngs of school kids.

The **Museu da História Natural** houses a rather dreary collection

Lisbon graffiti

Graffiti has long been a feature of Lisbon life – in the form of political protest under the Salazar regime – and the council's heritage department has given over certain city walls to be part of a Galeria de Arte Urbana, in which street art is encouraged. The annual urban art festival, O Bairro i o Mundo, has been credited with alleviating some of the problems of the Quinta do Mocho district north of the airport. The result is a dazzling array of graffiti all over the city, but particularly around the Bairro Alto and the Alcântara docks. Lisbon's best-known graffiti artist is Alexandre Farto, aka Vhils, whose large and striking works are often chiselled into brickwork using pneumatic drills.

Jardim Botânico

of stuffed animals, eggs and shells, though temporary exhibitions can be more diverting.

Jardim Botânico

MAP P.60, POCKET MAP H5
Rua Escola Politécnica 58 ℹ 213 921 800, ⓦ museus.ulisboa.pt. Daily: April–Sept 9am–8pm; Oct–March 9am–5pm. €2 gardens or €6 for combined ticket to Museus de História e da Ciência.

The lush **botanical gardens** are almost invisible from the surrounding streets and provide a tranquil escape from the city bustle. The Portuguese explorers introduced many plant species to Europe during the golden age of exploration and these gardens, laid out between 1858 and 1878, are packed with twenty thousand neatly labelled species from around the world. Shady paths lead downhill under towering palms and luxuriant shrubs past a "Lugartagis" greenhouse for breeding butterflies.

Palácio da Assembléia

MAP P.60, POCKET MAP H6
Rua de São Bento. Tram #28.
Below the Bairro Alto in the district of São Bento, you can't miss the late sixteenth-century Neoclassical facade of the **Palácio da Assembléia**. Formerly a Benedictine monastery, it was taken over by the government in 1834 and today houses the Assembléia da República, Portugal's **parliament**; it's not open to the public, though you can book a tour by special arrangement (ℹ 213 919 625, ⓦ parlamento.pt). Most visitors make do with the view of its steep white steps from tram #28 as it rattles along Calçada da Estrela, though it is worth exploring the earthy streets nearby. This was where Lisbon's black community put down roots – Rua do Poço dos Negros (Black Man's Well) takes its awful name from the corpses of slaves tossed into a hole here.

Casa Museu Amália Rodrigues

MAP P.60, POCKET MAP G6
Rua de São Bento 193 ℹ 213 971 896, ⓦ amaliarodrigues.pt. Daily 10am–6pm. €5. Bus #706 from Cais do Sodré, or a short walk from tram #28.

The daughter of an Alfama orange-seller, **Amália Rodrigues** was the undisputed queen of fado music until her death in 1999. The house where she lived since the 1950s has been kept as it was, and you can also admire original posters advertising her performances on stage and in the cinema, portraits by Portuguese artists and some of her personal possessions.

Shops

Cork & Co.

MAP P.60, POCKET MAP B12
Rua das Salgadeiras 10
ⓦ corkandcompany.pt. Mon–Sat
11am–8pm, Sun 5–9pm.
Portugal supplies around fifty
percent of the world's cork, and this
stylish shop displays the versatility
of the product with a range of
tasteful cork goods, from bags and
bracelets to umbrellas.

Embaixada

MAP P.60, POCKET MAP A10
Praça do Príncipe Real 26 ⓣ 963 309 154,
ⓦ www.embaixadalx.pt. Daily noon–8pm.
Housed in a former pseudo-Moorish
palace overlooking Praça do Príncipe
Real, this is a beautiful upmarket
emporium where boutiques showcase
Portugal's leading names in fashion.
There are designer clothes, shoes
and crafts along with temporary
exhibits and a café-bar-restaurant in
a wonderfully ornate room.

Solar Albuquerque

MAP P.60, POCKET MAP B10
Rua Dom Pedro V 70 ⓣ 213 465 522.
Mon–Fri 10am–7pm, Sat 10am–1pm.
Closed Sat in July and Aug.
A huge treasure-trove of antique
tiles, plates and ceramics dating
back to the sixteenth century –
great for a browse.

Restaurants

1° de Maio

MAP P.60, POCKET MAP B12
Rua da Atalaia 8 ⓣ 213 426 840. Mon–Fri
noon–3pm & 7–11pm, Sat noon–3pm.
Naked Chef-style food: simple slabs
of grilled fish and meat with boiled
veg and chips. You can watch
the cook through a hatch at the
back, adding to the theatrics of a
bustling, traditional *adega* (wine
cellar) with a low, arched ceiling.
Mains are around €10–12. Get
there early to be sure of a table.

Bistro 100 Maneiras

MAP P.60, POCKET MAP C11
Largo da Trindade 9 ⓣ 210 990 575.
Daily 7pm–2am.
In a fine Art Nouveau building
with film-inspired decor, Sarajevo-
born chef Ljubomir Stanisic
produces a fascinating mixture of
classy mains, such as sea urchin
with scrambled egg or spicy
octopus with *açorda* (€28), plus
comfort foods such as salmon
burgers and risotto (€18).

Bota Alta

MAP P.60, POCKET MAP B11
Trav da Queimada 37 ⓣ 213 427 959.
Mon–Fri noon–2.30pm & 7–10.30pm,
Sat 7–10.30pm.
Tavern decorated with old boots
(*botas*) and an eclectic picture
collection. It attracts queues for
its vast portions of sensibly priced,
traditional Portuguese food –
including *bacalhau com natas* (cod
cooked in cream) and fine cakes.
The tables are crammed in and it's
always packed; arrive before 8pm or
book in advance. Mains from €11.

Cervejaria Trindade

MAP P.60, POCKET MAP C11
Rua Nova da Trindade 20 ⓣ 213 423 506.
Daily noon–midnight.
The city's oldest beer-hall dates
from 1836. At busy times you'll be
shown to your table; at others find
a space in the original vaulted hall,
decorated with *azulejos*, depicting
the elements and seasons. Shellfish
is the speciality, though other fish
and meat dishes (from €12) are
lighter on the wallet. There is also
a patio garden and – a rarity – a
children's menu.

Comida de Santo

MAP P.60, POCKET MAP H6
Calçada Engenheiro Miguel Pais 39 ⓣ 213
963 339. Mon & Wed–Sun 12.30–3.30pm &
7.30pm–midnight; evenings only in Aug.
Late-opening Brazilian restaurant
serving cocktails and classic
dishes such as *feijoada a Brasileira*
(Brazilian bean stew) and a fantastic

ensopadinho de peixe (fish in coconut), along with some good vegetarian options. Mains €13–16.

Esplanada Cafe

MAP P.60, POCKET MAP A10
Praça do Príncipe Real ☎ 962 311 669. **Daily 9am–midnight.**

A good range of burgers, salads and tapas (€7–9) makes this an ideal and inexpensive lunch spot. The outdoor tables set under the trees get snapped up quickly, though the glass pavilion comes into its own when the weather turns. It's also a popular LGBTQ haunt.

La Paparrucha

MAP P.60, POCKET MAP B10
Rua Dom Pedro V 18–20 ☎ 213 425 333. **Mon–Fri noon–11.30pm, Sat & Sun 12.30–11.30pm.**

The best feature of this Argentinian restaurant is the fantastic back room and terrace offering superb views over the Baixa. The food is recommended too, with steaks, fish and pasta options. Mains from €14, with good-value lunchtime buffets from around €13.

O Cantinho do Bem Estar

MAP P.60, POCKET MAP C12
Rua do Norte 46 ☎ 213 464 265. **Tues–Sat 1–3pm & 7–11pm, Sun 7–11pm.**

Small and popular, the "canteen of well-being" lives up to its name: get there early to guarantee a place. From the menu, the rice dishes and generous salads are the best bet.

O Prego da Peixaria

MAP P.60, POCKET MAP H5
Rua Escola Politécnica 40 ☎ 213 471 356. **Daily 12.30pm–1am.**

Traditional *pregos* are steak sandwiches, but this fashionable restaurant has embraced a whole host of varieties. Choose from the likes of *bacalhau*, tuna, mushroom or salmon with octopus; all are delicious and around €9–13. There's a cool interior courtyard and fittings made from recycled materials.

Pharmacia

Páteo

MAP P.60, POCKET MAP C11
Bairro do Avillez, Rua Nova da Trinade 18 ☎ 215 830 290, ⓦ bairrodoavillez.pt. **Daily 12.30–3pm & 7pm–midnight.**

Top chef José Avillez has four lively restaurants in this artfully converted former monastery: *Páteo* is at the heart of the "patio", a beautiful balconied space beneath soaring roof lights. It specialises in fish and seafood plates, with sublime dishes such as garlic prawns, fish rice and tuna *escabeche*, as well as a handful of meat and vegetarian dishes.

Pharmacia

MAP P.60, POCKET MAP A12
Rua Marechal Saldanha 1 ☎ 213 462 146. **Tues–Sun 1pm–1am.**

Part of the Pharmaceutical Society and Museum, this traditional building on lawns facing the Tejo is a terrific spot for a quirky café-restaurant decked out with retro pharmacy fittings. The speciality here is tapas (from around €7). Enjoy daily specials in the evening, or just pop in for a drink.

Príncipe do Calhariz

MAP P.60, POCKET MAP B12
Calçado do Combro 28–30 ☎ 213 420
971. Mon–Fri & Sun noon–3pm &
7–10.30pm.

Here's a place that's reliable,
good value, has plenty of tables,
generous portions – and a local
buzz. Recommended are the *porco
Portuguesa* (fried pork cubes with
fried potatoes) and the salmon
steaks. Leave room for the rich
chocolate mousse. Mains from €9.

Tasca do Manel

MAP P.60, POCKET MAP B12
Rua da Barroca 24 ☎ 213 463 813. Daily
noon–3pm & 6.30–11.30pm.

One of the dying breed of
inexpensive *tascas*, still attracting a
largely local crowd for wholesome
dishes such as wild boar, grilled
salmon or bean stew from around
€10–12 with outdoor seats
in summer.

Tascardoso

MAP P.60, POCKET MAP A10
Rua Dom Pedro V 137 ☎ 213 427 578.
Mon–Sat noon–midnight.

Go through the stand-up bar
and head down the stairs to the
tiny eating area for excellent and
inexpensive tapas-style meats and
cheeses and good-value hot dishes
from around €7–12.

Terra

MAP P.60, POCKET MAP A10
Rua da Palmeira 15 ☎ 213 421 407.
Tues–Sun 12.30–3.30pm & 7.30–midnight.

Attractive vegetarian and vegan
restaurant with a lovely patio
garden, serving veggie versions of
classic Portuguese dishes. The all-
you-can-eat buffets are good value
at around €16; leave room for the
Italian ice creams.

Cafés

Lost In

MAP P.60, POCKET MAP B10
Rua Dom Pedro V 56 ☎ 917 759 282.
Mon 4pm–midnight, Tues–Sun 12.30pm–
midnight.

This little Indian-inspired café-
restaurant has a great terrace with
exhilarating views over town and
occasional live jazz. The menu
features prawn curry and veggie
burgers (€12–14), or just pop in
for a drink.

Lost In

Noobai

MAP P.60, POCKET MAP A12
Miradouro do Adamastor, Rua de Catarina
☎ 213 465 014, ⓦ noobaicafe.com.
Daily 10am–midnight.

Modern, jazzy café-restaurant
with a superb terrace just below
Miradouro de Santa Catarina.
Fabulous views complement the
inexpensive fresh juices, cocktails,
tapas, quiches and the like.

Tease

MAP P.60, POCKET MAP H6
Rua Nova da Piedade 15 ☎ 914 447 383,
ⓦ tease.pt. Daily 9am–8pm.

Specializing in amazing cupcakes
and chocolate goodies, this hip,
tiled café with jazzy sounds also
teases your tastebuds with juices,
smoothies and inexpensive light
lunches such as quiches and salads.

Bars and clubs

A Tasca Tequila Bar

MAP P.60, POCKET MAP C11
Trav da Queimada 13–15 ☎ 915 617 805.
Daily 6pm–2am.

Colourful, buzzy Mexican
bar with Latin sounds, which
caters to a good-time crowd
downing tequilas, margaritas and
Brazilian *caipirinhas*.

Chafariz do Vinho Enoteca

MAP P.60, POCKET MAP A10
Rua da Mãe de Água ☎ 213 422 079.
Tues–Sun 6pm–1am.

This extraordinary wine bar is set
in the bowels of a nineteenth-
century bathhouse whose
underground tunnels once piped
water into Lisbon. The bar
offers a long list of Portuguese
wines, which you can enjoy with
regional breads and assorted
petiscos (snacks) such as oysters
or dates with bacon (€6–11).
It gets busy at weekends so it's
best to reserve if you want to eat,
though you can always squeeze
in for a drink or sit at one of the
outside tables.

Chafariz do Vinho Enoteca

Cinco Lounge

MAP P.60, POCKET MAP A11
Rua Ruben A. Leitão 17a
ⓦ cincolounge.com. Daily 9pm–2am.

A New York-style cocktail lounge
run by Brits in the heart of Lisbon
– there are over a hundred cocktails
to choose from; go for one of the
wacky fruit concoctions (anyone
for gin, lime and dandelion?) while
sinking into one of the enormous
comfy sofas.

Clube da Esquina

MAP P.60, POCKET MAP B12
Rua da Barroca 30 ☎ 929 092 742.
Mon–Thurs 7pm–2am, Fri & Sat 7pm–3am,
Sun 9pm–2am.

Buzzing little corner bar with ancient
radios on the walls and DJs spinning
discs. Attracts a young crowd
enjoying vast measures of spirits.

Janela da Atalaia

MAP P.60, POCKET MAP B11
Rua da Atalaia 160 ☎ 213 465 988.
Mon–Sat 7pm–3am.

A fine old bar with two rooms,
inexpensive drinks and laidback
sounds, usually world music. Most
Wednesdays there's a band, often
salsa/Brazilian.

Majong

MAP P.60, POCKET MAP B12
Rua da Atalaia 3 ⓘ 213 421 039.
Daily 8pm–2am.

At the bottom of the Bairro Alto and traditionally a place to start an evening before moving on up. It's a great space, with plain white tiles and a rough wooden bar juxtaposed with modern Chinese motifs – the clientele are similarly eclectic.

Maria Caxuxa

MAP P.60, POCKET MAP B12
Rua da Barroca 12 ⓘ 965 039 094.
Mon–Sat 6pm–2am.

This arty lounge-bar has plenty of space for big sofas and eclectic decor – including record players and aged machinery – though these get lost in the crowds when the DJ pumps up the volume as the evening progresses.

Park

MAP P.60, POCKET MAP A12
Calçada do Combro 58 ⓘ 215 914 011.
Tues–Sat 1pm–2am, Sun 1pm–8pm.

Reached via a poky entrance inside a car park, this chic rooftop bar

comes as quite a surprise. There are potted plants and trees, great cocktails and bar snacks, and a stunning view across the river. At weekends there are often guest DJs and cultural events.

Pavilhão Chinês

MAP P.60, POCKET MAP B10
Rua Dom Pedro V 89–91 ⓘ 213 424 729.
Daily 6pm–2am.

Once a nineteenth-century tea and coffee merchants' shop, this is now a quirky bar set in a series of comfy rooms, including a pool room. Most are lined with mirrored cabinets containing a bizarre range of 4000 artefacts from around the world, including a cabinet of model trams. There's waiter service and the usual drinks are supplemented by a long list of cocktails.

Portas Largas

MAP P.60, POCKET MAP B11
Rua da Atalaia 103–105 ⓘ 218 466 379.
Daily 8pm–2am.

The bar's *portas largas* (big doors) are usually thrown wide open, inviting the neighbourhood into

Pavilhão Chinês

Solar do Vinho do Porto

this friendly black-and-white-tiled *adega* (wine cellar). There are cheapish drinks, music from fado to pop (sometimes live), and a young, mixed gay and straight clientele, which spills onto the streets.

Solar do Vinho do Porto

MAP P.60, POCKET MAP B11
Rua de São Pedro de Alcântara 45
☎ 213 475 707, ⓦ www.ivp.pt. Mon–Fri
11am–midnight, Sat 3pm–midnight.
The eighteenth-century Palácio Ludovice is home to the Lisbon branch of the Port Wine Institute, responsible for promoting one of Portugal's most famous exports. Visitors are lured in with over three hundred types of port, starting at around €3 a glass and rising to some €25 for a glass of forty-year-old J.W. Burmester. Drinks (as well as hams and cheeses) are served at low tables in the mansion's stylishly designed interior. The waiters are notoriously snooty, but it's still a good place to kick off an evening.

Music venues

Alface Hall

MAP P.60, POCKET MAP C11
Rua do Norte 96 ☎ 213 433 293.
Daily 4pm–midnight.
This quirky little café-bar is housed in a former printworks. Now part of a hostel and filled with retro chairs and artefacts, its high ceilings and comfy sofas make it an ideal place to hang out for live jazz and blues, daily from 9pm.

Tasca do Chico

MAP P.60, POCKET MAP B12
Rua do Diário de Notícias 39
☎ 961 339 696. Daily 7pm–1.30am.
Atmospheric little bar filled with football scarves (a fine spot for a drink), which morphs into a very popular fado bar on Mondays and Wednesdays, when crowds pack in to hear moving fado from 8pm.

Estrela, Lapa and Santos

West of the Bairro Alto sits the leafy district of Estrela, best known for its gardens and enormous basilica. To the south lies opulent Lapa, Lisbon's diplomatic quarter, sheltering some of its top hotels. Sumptuous mansions and grand embassy buildings peer out majestically towards the Tejo. The superb Museu Nacional de Arte Antiga below here is Portugal's national gallery, while down on the riverfront, Santos is promoted as "the district of design" with some of the city's coolest shops.

Basílica and Jardim da Estrela

MAP P.73, POCKET MAP G6
Largo da Estrela. Church Daily 7.30am–1pm & 3–8pm. Free. Roof visits Mon–Sat 10am–6pm. €4. Tram #28 or #25.

The impressive **Basílica da Estrela** is a vast monument to late eighteenth-century Neoclassicism. Constructed by

Jardim da Estrela

order of Queen Maria I (whose tomb lies within), and completed in 1790, its landmark white dome can be seen from much of the city. You can visit the flat roof (via 140 steep stone steps) for fine views over the western suburbs, and also walk round the inside of the dome to peer down at the church interior 25m below. Opposite is the **Jardim da Estrela** (daily; free), one of the city's most enjoyable gardens with a pond-side café and a well-equipped children's playground.

Cemitério dos Ingleses

MAP P.73, POCKET MAP G6
Rua São Jorge 6 ☎ 213 906 248. Mon–Fri 10.30am–1pm. Free. Tram #28 or #25.

"**The English Cemetery**" is actually a cemetery for all Protestants, founded in 1717. Here, among the cypresses and tombs of various expatriates, lie the remains of Henry Fielding. He came to Lisbon hoping the climate would improve his failing health, but his inability to recuperate may have influenced his verdict on Lisbon as "the nastiest city in the world".

Lapa

MAP P.73, POCKET MAP F7
From Estrela tram #25 skirts past the well-heeled district of **Lapa** on its way down to the waterfront. Lapa is the most desired address

Museu Nacional de Arte Antiga

in the city and though it contains no sights as such, it is worth wandering around to admire the stunning mansions. A good route is to follow the tram tracks from Estrela and turn right into Rua do Sacramento à Lapa, past fantastic embassy buildings. Turn left into Rua do Pau da Bandeira past the *Olissippo Lapa Palace* hotel (if you have the funds, have a drink at the bar). From here, go left into Rua do Prior and right into Rua do Conde and it's a ten-minute walk downhill to the Museu Nacional de Arte Antiga (see below).

Museu Nacional de Arte Antiga

MAP P.73, POCKET MAP G8
Rua das Janelas Verdes 95. Bus #760 from Praça da Figueira, #727 from Belém or a short walk from tram #25 ☎ 213 912 800, Ⓦ museudearteantiga.pt. Tues–Sun 10am–6pm. €6.

The **Museu Nacional de Arte Antiga** features the largest collection of Portuguese fifteenth- and sixteenth-century paintings in the country, European art from the fourteenth century to the present day and a rich display of applied art. All of this is well exhibited in a tastefully converted seventeenth-century palace once owned by the Marquês de Pombal. The museum uses ten "reference points" to guide you round the collection. The principal highlight is **Nuno Gonçalves's altarpiece** dedicated to St Vincent (1467–70), a brilliantly marshalled composition depicting Lisbon's patron saint receiving homage from all ranks of its citizens, their faces appearing remarkably modern. The other main highlight is Hieronymus Bosch's stunningly gruesome *Temptation of St Anthony* in room 57 (don't miss the image on the back of the painting, showing the arrest of Christ). Elsewhere, seek out the altar panel depicting the *Resurrection* by

Santos district

Raphael; Francisco de Zurbarán's *The Twelve Apostles;* a small statue of a nymph by Auguste Rodin; and works by Dürer, Holbein, Cranach (particularly *Salome*), Fragonard and Josefa de Óbidos, considered one of Portugal's greatest female painters.

The **Oriental art** collection shows how the Portuguese were influenced by overseas designs encountered during the sixteenth century. There is inlaid furniture from Goa, Turkish and Syrian *azulejos*, Qing Dynasty porcelain and a fantastic series of late sixteenth-century Japanese *namban* screens (room 14), depicting the Portuguese landing at Nagasaki. The Japanese regarded the Portuguese traders as southern barbarians (*namban*) with large noses – hence their Pinocchio-like features. The museum extends over the remains of the sixteenth-century St Albert monastery, most

of which was razed during the 1755 earthquake, although its beautiful chapel can still be seen today, downstairs by the main entrance. Don't miss the garden café, either (see page 75).

Museu da Marioneta

MAP P.73, POCKET MAP G7
Rua da Esperança 146. Tram #25 then a short walk ☏ 213 942 810, ⊛ museudamarioneta. pt. Tues–Sun 10am–6pm. €5, children €3, free Sun 10am–2pm.

Contemporary and historical **puppets** from around the world are displayed in this former eighteenth-century convent and demonstrated in a well-laid-out **museum**. Highlights include shadow puppets from Turkey and Indonesia, string marionettes, Punch and Judy-style puppets and almost life-sized, faintly disturbing modern figures by Portuguese puppeteer Helena Vaz, which are anything but cute. There are also video displays and projections, masks from Africa and Asia, while the final room exhibits Wallace and Gromit-style plasticine figures with demonstrations on how they are manipulated for films.

Santos

MAP P.73, POCKET MAP G7
Santos was traditionally a run-down riverside area of factories and warehouses where people only ventured after dark because of its nightclubs. Over the years, artists and designers moved into the inexpensive and expansive warehouse spaces, and now Santos has a reputation as the city's designer heartland. Its riverside streets are not particularly alluring, but you can see many of the country's top designers showcasing their products in various shops and galleries. Fashionable bars and restaurants have followed in their wake, though the area around the Museu da Marioneta retains an earthy, villagey feel to its cobbled backstreets.

ESTRELA, LAPA AND SANTOS

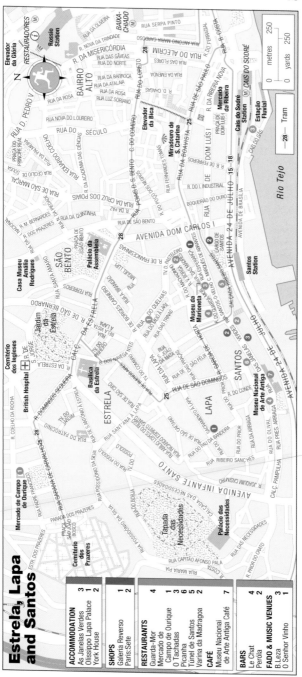

Estrela, Lapa and Santos

ACCOMMODATION
As Janelas Verdes	3
Olissippo Lapa Palace	1
York House	2

SHOPS
Galeria Reverso	1
Paris:Sete	2

RESTAURANTS
Guarda-Mor	4
Mercado de Campo de Ourique	1
O Tachadas	3
Picanha	6
Túnel de Santos	5
Varina da Madragoa	2

CAFÉ
Museu Nacional de Arte Antiga Café	7

BARS
Le Chat	4
Perola	2

FADO & MUSIC VENUES
B.Leza	3
O Senhor Vinho	1

Shops

Galeria Reverso

MAP P.73, POCKET MAP H7

Rua da Esperança 59–61 ☎ 213 951 407.
Tues & Thurs 11am–7pm, Wed
& Fri 2–7pm.

Jewellery workshop and gallery
managed by well-known
Portuguese designer Paula Crespo,
whose big, heavy jewellery is eye-
catching. International designers
also feature, many using unusual
materials such as rubber and wood,
though to buy anything you'll need
a deep purse.

Paris:Sete

MAP P.73, POCKET MAP H7

Largo Vitorino Damásio 2 ☎ 213 933 170,
Ⓦ paris-sete.com. Mon–Fri 10am–7pm,
Sat 10.30am–5pm.

Bright, white space selling
designer furniture and curios, with
heavyweight names such as Charles
and Ray Eames and Philippe Starck
behind some of them.

Restaurants

Guarda-Mor

MAP P.73, POCKET MAP G7

Rua do Guarda-Mor 8 ☎ 213 928 663.
Tues–Fri 12.30–3pm & 7.30pm–midnight,
Sat 7.30pm–midnight.

One of Santos' more local options
serving great, mid-priced dishes
such as *pataniscas de bacalhau*
(dried cod cakes), *açorda de
gambas* (prawns in bread sauce)
and *gambas fritas com limão*
(prawns fried in lemon). Also has
occasional live fado (Wed). Mains
from €14.

Mercado de Campo de Ourique

MAP P.73, POCKET MAP F6

Rua Coelho da Rocha 104 ☎ 211 323
701. Mon–Thurs 10am–11pm, Fri & Sat
10am–1am.

This wonderful 1930s building
has been given a revamp and

now not only sells fish, fruit and
veg, but also shelters around
twenty *tasquinhas* (small food
stalls) serving pastries, sushi,
petiscos, burgers and seafood.
There are also bars (gin cocktails,
flavoured teas and the like) and
occasional live entertainment in
the evenings.

O Tachadas

MAP P.73, POCKET MAP G7

Rua da Esperança 178 ☎ 213 976 689.
Tues–Sun noon–3pm & 6.30–11pm.

Arrive early to guarantee a table
at this very popular, good-value
local, where people come for vast
portions of beautifully grilled
steaks, chicken, pork or fish, best
washed down with Alentejan wines.
Mains start at around €12, but they
are usually large enough to share
between two people.

Picanha

MAP P.73, POCKET MAP G8

Rua das Janelas Verdes 96 ☎ 213 975 401.
Mon–Sat 12.30–3.30pm & 8–11pm, Sun
12.30–3.30pm.

This ornately tiled restaurant
specializes in *picanha* (strips of
beef in garlic sauce) accompanied
by black-eyed beans, salad and
potatoes. Great if this appeals
to you, since for a fixed-price of
around €20 you can eat all you
want; otherwise forget it, as it's all
that's on offer.

Túnel de Santos

MAP P.73, POCKET MAP G7

Largo de Santos 1 ☎ 912 151 850.
Mon–Sat noon–4am.

Lively, modern café-restaurant with
brick vaulted ceilings and outdoor
seating facing the square, attracting
a young crowd for inexpensive
grills, snacks and salads.

Varina da Madragoa

MAP P.73, POCKET MAP G7

Rua das Madres 34 ☎ 213 965 533.
Tues–Sun 12.30–3.30pm & 8–11pm.

A delightfully simple local that's
hosted the likes of fomer US

President Jimmy Carter and Portuguese PM José Sócrates – and it's easy to see why they liked it: a lovely, traditional restaurant with grape-motif *azulejos* on the walls and a menu featuring dishes such as *bacalhau*, trout and steaks. Desserts include a splendid almond ice cream with hot chocolate sauce. Mains from €10.

Café

Museu Nacional de Arte Antiga Café

MAP P.73, POCKET MAP G8
Rua das Janelas Verdes 95 ⓘ 213 912 860, Tues–Sun 10am–5.30pm.
There's no need to visit the museum to use its fantastic café – go in through the museum exit opposite Largo Dr J de Figueiredo and head to the basement. Lunches and drinks can be enjoyed in a superb garden studded with statues and overlooking Lisbon's docks.

Bars

Le Chat

MAP P.73, POCKET MAP F8
Jardim 9 de Abril ⓘ 213 963 668. Mon–Sat 12.30pm–2am & Sun 12.30pm–midnight.
A modern, glass-sided bar-restaurant adjacent to the Museu Nacional de Arte Antiga, *Le Chat* has a terrific terrace which gazes over the docks and Ponte 25 de Abril. Great at any time of the day, it's a particularly fine spot for a cocktail or sundowner.

Pérola

MAP P.73, POCKET MAP G7
Calçada Ribeiro dos Santos 25
ⓘ 917 745 516. Daily 10am–4am.
A small local bar given a makeover, with table football to play and a little dining area to the back. Most hole up in the front room for inexpensive drinks and good music.

Fado and music venues

B.Leza

MAP P.73, POCKET MAP A14
Cais da Ribeira Nova Armazém B
ⓘ 210 106 837. Wed–Sat 10.30pm–4am, Sun 6pm–2am.
A great African club, with live music, poetry nights, *kizomba* evenings and occasional dance lessons on offer, though you'd be hard pushed to outshine the regulars.

O Senhor Vinho

MAP P.73, POCKET MAP G7
Rua do Meio à Lapa 18 ⓘ 213 972 681, ⓦ srvinho.com. Mon–Sat 8pm–2am.
In the fashionable Madragoa district, this famous fado club features some of the best singers in Portugal (from 9pm), hence the high prices (around €50 a head). Reservations are advised.

Le Chat

Alcântara and the docks

Loomed over by the enormous Ponte 25 de Abril suspension bridge, Alcântara has a decidedly industrial hue, with a tangle of flyovers and cranes from the docks dominating the skyline. The area is well known for its nightlife, thanks mainly to its dockside warehouse conversions that shelter cafés and restaurants. It also hosts a couple of fine museums, both tipping their hats to Portugal's historic links with the Far East and there's an attractive riverside promenade. To get to the docks, take a train from Cais do Sodré to Alcântara-Mar or tram #15.

Museu do Oriente

MAP P.78, POCKET MAP E8
Avda de Brasília ☎ 213 585 200,
Ⓦ museudooriente.pt. Tues–Sun
10am–6pm, late opening Fri until 10pm.
€6, free Fri 6–10pm.

Owned by the powerful Orient Foundation, this spacious **museum** traces the cultural links that Portugal has built up with its former colonies in Macao, India, East Timor and other Asian countries. Housed in an enormous 1930s Estado Novo building,

highlights of the extensive collection include valuable nineteenth-century Chinese porcelain, an amazing array of seventeenth-century Chinese snuff boxes and, from the same century, Japanese armour and entire carved pillars from Goa. The top floor is given over to displays on the Gods of Asia, featuring a bright collection of religious costumes and shrines used in Bali and Vietnam together with Taoist altars, statues of

Museu do Oriente

Doca de Santo Amaro

Buddha, some fine Japanese Shinto masks and Indonesian shadow puppets. Vivid images of Hindu gods Shiva, Ganesh the elephant god and Kali the demon are counterbalanced by some lovely Thai amulets. There is also a decent top-floor restaurant serving good food.

Doca de Santo Amaro

MAP P.78, POCKET MAP D9

Just west of the Doca de Alcântara lies the more intimate **Doca de Santo Amaro**, nestling right under the humming traffic and rattling trains crossing Ponte 25 de Abril. This small, almost completely enclosed, marina is filled with bobbing sailing boats and lined with tastefully converted warehouses. Its cluster of international cafés and restaurants are pricier than usual for Lisbon but the constant comings and goings of the Tejo provide plenty of free entertainment to diners. Leaving Doca de Santo Amaro at its western side, you can pick up a pleasant riverside path that leads all the way to Belém (see page 82), twenty minutes' walk away.

Ponte 25 de Abril and the Pilar 7 Bridge Experience

MAP P.78. POCKET MAP D9.
Avenida da India ☎ 211 117 880. Daily: April–Sept 10am–8pm; Oct–March 10am–6pm. €6.

Resembling the Golden Gate Bridge in San Francisco, the hugely impressive **Ponte 25 de Abril** was opened in 1966 as a vital link between Lisbon and the southern banks of the Tejo. Around 2.3km in length, the bridge rises to 70m above the river, though its main pillars are nearly 200m tall. It was originally named Ponte de Salazar after the dictatorial prime minister who ruled Portugal with an iron fist from 1932 to 1968, but took its present name to mark the date of the revolution that overthrew Salazar's regime in 1974. The dizzying **Pilar 7 Bridge Experience** offers the opportunity to ascend 70m up one of the bridge's pillars to a glass-encased platform for a close-up look at the thundering traffic and for stunning views across the western riverfront. Inside, an exhibition space traces the history of the bridge using models and multimedia, including a somewhat grainy projection room detailing how three thousand workers built the bridge using 55,000km of steel wire. For an extra €1.50, you can experience a virtual-reality recreation of how maintenance workers carry out repairs on the central pillars, a hairy 200m above the river. Note that only 100 people can visit at any one time (40 on the viewpoint).

Museu do Centro Científico e Cultural de Macau

MAP P.78, POCKET MAP C9
Rua da Junqueira 30 ☎ 213 617 570, W www.cccm.pt. Tues–Sun 10am–6pm. €3, free Sun 10am–2pm.

This attractively laid-out **museum** is dedicated to Portugal's historical **trading links** with the Orient and, specifically, its former colony of Macao, which was handed back to Chinese rule in 1999. There are model boats and audio displays detailing early sea voyages, as well as various historic journals and artefacts, including a seventeenth-

century portable wooden altar, used by travelling clergymen. Upstairs, exhibitions of Chinese art from the sixteenth to the nineteenth centuries show off ornate collections of porcelain, silverware and applied art, most notably an impressive array of opium pipes and ivory boxes.

Museu da Carris

MAP P.78, POCKET MAP D8
Rua 1° de Maio 101 ☎ 213 613 087, W museu.carris.pt. Mon–Sat 10am–6pm. €4.

This engagingly quirky and ramshackle **museum** traces the history of Lisbon's **public transport**, from the earliest trams and street lifts to the development of the metro. There are three zones, the first with evocative black-and-white photos, uniforms and models. You then hop on a real tram dating from 1901 which takes you to a warehouse filled with historic trams, and then on to another warehouse with ancient buses and models

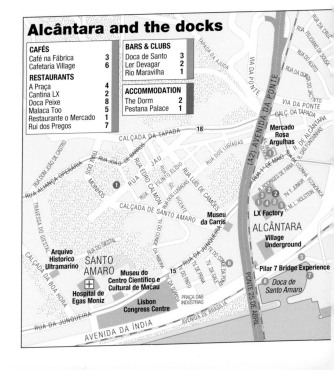

Alcântara and the docks

CAFÉS		
Café na Fábrica		3
Cafetaria Village		6
RESTAURANTS		
A Praça		4
Cantina LX		2
Doca Peixe		8
Malaca Too		5
Restaurante o Mercado		1
Rui dos Pregos		7

BARS & CLUBS		
Doca de Santo		3
Ler Devagar		2
Rio Maravilha		1
ACCOMMODATION		
The Dorm		2
Pestana Palace		1

of metro trains. It's great fun for kids especially, who can clamber on board and pretend to drive the vehicles. The bottom of the site also has the eye-catching Village Underground, a bizarre medley of old shipping containers and double-decker buses now given over to work spaces for writers and artists.

LX Factory

MAP P.78, POCKET MAP D8
Rua Rodrigues Faria 103 ☎ 213 143 399,
Ⓦ lxfactory.com.

Below Ponte 25 de Abril, this former nineteenth-century industrial estate is now the place to test Lisbon's creative pulse. The factories and warehouses have turned into a mini-district of workshops and studios for the city's go-getters, along with a series of superb boutiques, shops, cafés and bars set in fashionably run-down urban spaces. Sunday is a good time to visit, with a

LX Factory

lively flea market (noon–7pm) and many places open for brunch: **LX Factory**'s Open Days take place throughout the year, featuring shows, live music and film screenings (check website for details), and in September it hosts the Nova Batida festival (Ⓦ novabatida.com).

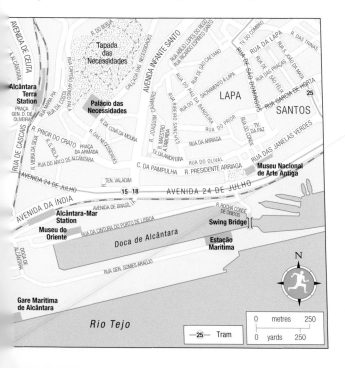

Cafés

Café na Fábrica

MAP P.78, POCKET MAP D8
LX Factory, Rua Rodrigues Faria 103
☏ 967 382 848. Mon–Fri 9am–9pm, Sat
11am–10.30pm, Sun 11am–7pm.
Set in a small but cosy wooden
warehouse, this arty space is very
popular for lunch, with wraps,
quiches, baguettes and salads from
around €7. There are also a few
outdoor tables.

Cafetaria Village

MAP P.78, POCKET MAP D9
Village Underground, Rua 1° de Maio 103
☏ 215 583 469. Daily noon–6pm (closes
8pm in summer).
Grab a sandwich (€5–7), salad or
dish of the day at the café inside
Village Underground (see page
79), which is inside an old
double-decker bus. There are tables
inside or out, where you can sit
with Lisbon's creative set.

Restaurants

A Praça

MAP P.78, POCKET MAP D8
LX Factory, Edifício H, Espaço 001
☏ 210 991 792. Daily 12.30–10.30pm.
One of the larger restaurants in
LX Factory, a hip spot with an
open kitchen serving a range of
dishes, including pasta, steaks and
seafood from €12–15. It also does
good cocktails.

Cantina LX

MAP P.78, POCKET MAP D8
LX Factory, Rua Rodrigues Faria 103
☏ 213 628 239. Daily noon–11pm.
Upcycled furniture and bench-
like tables in a spacious former
warehouse make this a hip spot.
Great breakfasts, snacks and daily
specials which usually focus on
healthy salads from around €10.

Doca Peixe

MAP P.78, POCKET MAP D9
Armazém 14, Doca de Santo Amaro
☏ 213 973 556, ⓦ docapeixe.com.
Daily 12.30–11.30pm.
You'll need a deep wallet to eat at
this fish restaurant (mains from
€16), but with a counter groaning
under the weight of fresh fish, you
won't leave disappointed. They
also serve a great prawn curry and
sublime lobster rice with clams.

Malaca Too

MAP P.78, POCKET MAP D8
LX Factory, Rua Rodrigues Faria 103,
Edifício G-03 ☏ 213 477 082. Daily
12.30–3pm & 7.30pm–11pm.
This fantastic space has tables
wedged between giant old printing
presses – a surprising backdrop for

A Praça

fresh, oriental cuisine ranging from wanton soup and green curries to fresh fish, from around €12.

Restaurante o Mercado

MAP P.78, POCKET MAP D8
Mercado Rosa Agulhas, Rua Leão de Oliveira, Loja 25 ☎ 213 649 113. Mon–Sat noon–3pm & 7–midnight, Sun noon–5pm.
On three floors by the market building – and Lisbon's markets are always worth a call – this is a great place to have a hearty meal. The ingredients don't have far to travel: the fish and vegetables are day-fresh, and there's a long list of grilled meats and seafood, including a fine seafood pasta. Mains €12–14.

Rui dos Pregos

MAP P.78, POCKET MAP D9
Passeio Doca de Santo Amaro ☎ 967 723 483. Tues–Sat 11am–2am, Sun 11am–midnight.
One of the less pricey options set to one side of the docks, with appealing outdoor tables. The speciality here is *pregos* (beef sandwiches), with different varieties from €8.

Bars and clubs

Doca de Santo

MAP P.78, POCKET MAP D8
Armazém CP, Doca de Santo Amaro ☎ 213 942 410. Mon–Thurs & Sun 9am–midnight, Fri & Sat 9am–2am.
Though it's located slightly away from the river, this palm-fringed venue is worth seeking out; there's an enticing cocktail bar on the esplanade, while the restaurant inside serves well-priced modern Portuguese food (grilled fish and meats with pasta or couscous). From €10.

Ler Devagar

MAP P.78, POCKET MAP D8
LX Factory, Rua Rodrigues Faria 103, Edifício G-03 ☎ 213 259 992, ⊚ lerdevagar. com. Mon noon–9pm, Tues–Thurs noon–

Ler Devagar

midnight, Fri & Sat noon–2am, Sun 11am–9pm.
Primarily a wonderful arts bookshop, with shelves reaching an old printing press, this also has a corner café-bar, a great place to sample Portuguese wines by the glass. It also hosts exhibits and occasional live music.

Rio Maravilha

MAP P.78, POCKET MAP D8
LX Factory, Rua Rodrigues Faria 103, Edifício 1 entrada 3 ☎ 966 028 229. Tues–Sun 10am–2am.
Take the rickety lift or unpromising stairwell to the top of this industrial warehouse to discover a cool bar-restaurant with a fabulous roof terrace, where you can sit on multicoloured chairs and sip cocktails. There are fine views over the river from below a rainbow-coloured statue of a woman, mirroring the statue of Cristo Rei opposite.

Belém and Ajuda

With its maritime history and attractive riverside location, Belém (pronounced ber-layng) is understandably one of Lisbon's most popular suburbs. It was from Belém that Vasco da Gama famously set sail for India in 1497. The monastery subsequently built here – the Mosteiro dos Jerónimos – stands as a testament to his triumphant discovery of a sea route to the Orient, which initiated the beginning of a Portuguese golden age. Along with the monastery and the landmark Torre de Belém, the suburb boasts a group of small museums, including the fantastic Berardo Collection of modern art. Just to the northeast of Belém is Ajuda, famed for its palace and ancient botanical gardens. Higher still lies the extensive parkland of Monsanto, Lisbon's largest green space.

Praça do Império

MAP P.84, POCKET MAP C4

The formal walkways and gardens that make up **Praça do Império** are laid out over Belém's former beach. It's a popular spot, especially on Saturday mornings, when there are often weddings taking place at the monastery, whose photocalls invariably spill out into the square. The seventeenth-century buildings along Rua Vieira Portuense are now mostly restaurants with outdoor seating; as a rule, the further east you head, the better value they become.

Praça do Império

Belém transport

You can reach Belém on tram #15 (signed Algés), which runs from Praça da Figueira via Praça do Comércio (20min). Ask at the ticket offices of the main sites about combined tickets that can save money on entry to the main attractions, which all attract long queues in the summer. You can also take a hop-on, hop-off bus tour around the suburb's main sights, including the Ponte 25 Abril (☎211 117 880; daily hourly; April–Oct 10am–6pm; Nov–March 10am–5pm; €5). Alternatively, hire bikes (Daily 10am–7pm, Sat & Sun 9.30am–8pm, 7pm in winter, €4.50/1hr; ⊕biclas.com) from a kiosk 5min east of the MAAT (see page 87).

Jardim do Ultramar and Presidência da República

MAP P.84, POCKET MAP C4
Garden entrance on Calçada do Galvão
☎213 609 660, ⊕www2.iict.pt. Daily:
May–Oct 10am–6pm; Sept–April
10am–5pm. €2.

The leafy **Jardim do Ultramar** is an oasis of hothouses, ponds and towering palms, a lovely place for a walk. In the southeastern corner lies the President's official residence, the pink **Presidência da República**, which opens for guided visits on Saturdays (entrance on Praça Afonso de Albuquerque; 10.30am–4.30pm, €5; ⊕museu.presidencia.pt).

Museu de Arte Popular

MAP P.84, POCKET MAP B5
Avda de Brasília ☎213 011 282,
⊕museuartepopular.wordpress.com.
Daily 10am–8pm. €2.50, free first Sun of the month.

This charming **museum** chronicles Portugal's **folk art**, from beautiful wood and cork toys to ceramics, rugs and fascinating traditional costumes, including amazing cloaks from the Trás-os-Montes region.

Mosteiro dos Jerónimos

MAP P.84, POCKET MAP C4
Praça do Império ☎213 620 034,
⊕mosteirojeronimos.pt. Tues–Sun: May–Sept 10am–6pm; Oct–April 10am–5.30pm; restricted access on Sat mornings and during Mass. €10.

If there's one building that symbolizes the Golden Age of the Portuguese discoveries, it's the **Mosteiros dos Jerónimos**, which is also considered to be the first ever Manueline building. Now a designated UNESCO World Heritage Site, the monastery and its adjacent church were built to fulfill a promise that Portugal's king, Dom Manuel, made, should Vasco da Gama return safely from his inaugural voyage to India in 1498. Construction began in 1502 under the architect Diogo de Boitaca.

Appropriately, Vasco da Gama's tomb now lies just inside the fantastically embellished entrance to the church. Crowned by an elaborate medley of statues, including that of the famed Henry the Navigator, the 32-metre-high entrance was designed by the Spaniard João de Castilho, who took over the building of the church in 1517. The interior is even more dazzling, displaying the maritime influences typical of Manueline architecture – the escutcheons on its ceiling come from the actual ships that sailed the voyages of exploration. The church also contains the tomb of Luís de Camões (1527–1570), considered Portugal's greatest poet and recorder of the discoveries, alongside the tombs of a number of former presidents and dignitaries.

Equally impressive is the adjacent monastery, gathered

round sumptuously vaulted cloisters with nautical symbols carved into the honey-coloured limestone. You can still see the twelve niches where navigators stopped for confessionals before their voyages, until the Hieronymite monks were forced out during the dissolution of 1833. In 2007, the monastery was once again influential in blessing future trade: the Treaty of Lisbon was signed here to cement the format of the European Union.

Museu de Arqueologia

MAP P.84, POCKET MAP C4
Praça do Império ☎ 213 620 000,
ⓦ museuarqueologia.gov.pt. Tues–Sun 10am–6pm. €5, free first Sun of the month.
Housed in a neo-Manueline extension to the monastery added in 1850, the **archeology museum** has a small section on Egyptian antiquities dating from 6000

BC, but concentrates mainly on Portuguese archeological finds. It's a sparse collection reprieved by coins and jewellery through the ages, along with a few fine Roman mosaics.

Museu da Marinha

MAP P.84, POCKET MAP B4
Praça do Império ☎ 213 620 019,
ⓦ museu.marinha.pt. Tues–Sun: May–Sept 10am–6pm; Oct–April 10am–5pm. €6.50, free first Sun of the month.
In the west wing of the monastery extension is an absorbing and gargantuan **maritime museum**, packed not only with models of ships, naval uniforms and artefacts from Portugal's Oriental colonies, but also with real vessels – among them fishing boats and sumptuous state barges, plus early seaplanes. Much of the museum's collection comes from that of King Luís I (1861–1889), who was a keen oceanographer.

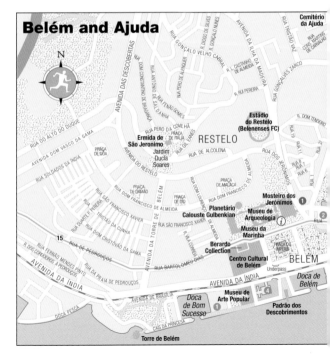

Centro Cultural de Belém

MAP P.84, POCKET MAP B4

Praça do Império ☎ 213 612 400, ⓦ ccb.pt.

The stylish, pink marble **Centro Cultural de Belém** was built to host Lisbon's 1992 presidency of the European Union. It's now one of the city's main cultural centres, containing the Berardo Collection (see below) and hosting regular photography and art exhibitions, as well as concerts and shows.

Berardo Collection

MAP P.84, POCKET MAP B4

Entrance via Centro Cultural de Belém, Praça do Império ☎ 213 612 878, ⓦ museuberardo.pt. Daily 10am–7pm. €5, free on Sat.

As impressive as Belém's historical monuments is this unique **collection of modern art** amassed by wealthy Madeiran Joe Berardo, Portugal's answer to Charles Saatchi or François Pinault. You can enjoy some of the world's top modern

Berardo Collection

ACCOMMODATION	
Jéronimos 8	1

RESTAURANTS	
Floresta de Belém	3
Portugália	4
Solar do Embaixador	1

CAFÉ	
Pastéis de Belém	2

BAR	
Á Margem	1

— 18 — Tram

0	metres	250
0	yards	250

Rio Tejo

Torre de Belém

artists, though not all of the vast collection is on display at the same time. Depending on when you visit, you may see Eric Fischl's giant panels of sunbathers; Andy Warhol's distinctive *Judy Garland*; and Chris Ofili's *Adoration of Captain Shit*, made with genuine dung. Portugal's Paula Rego is well represented – *The Past and Present* and *The Barn* are particularly strong. Francis Bacon, David Hockney, Picasso, Míro, Man Ray, Max Ernst and Mark Rothko also feature, along with various video artists.

Padrão dos Descobrimentos

MAP P.84, POCKET MAP C5
Avda de Brasília, reached via an underpass beneath the Avda da Índia ☎ 213 031 950, ⓦ padraodosdescobrimentos.pt. Daily: March–Sept 10am–7pm; Oct–Feb 10am–6pm. €5.

The **Padrão dos Descobrimentos** (Monument to the Discoveries) is a 54m-high, caravel-shaped slab of concrete erected in 1960 to commemorate the 500th anniversary of the death of Henry the Navigator. A large and detailed statue of Henry appears at the head of a line of statues that feature King Alfonso V, Luís de Camões, Vasco da Gama and other Portuguese heroes. Inside is a small exhibition space which often features displays on Lisbon's history – the entrance fee also includes a ride in the lift providing fine views of the Tejo and the Torre de Belém. Just in front of the monument, tourists pose on the marble pavement which is decorated with a map of the world charting the routes taken by the great Portuguese explorers.

Torre de Belém

MAP P.84, POCKET MAP A5
Avda de Brasília ☎ 213 620 034, ⓦ torrebelem.gov.pt. Tues–Sun: May–Sept 10am–6.30pm; Oct–April 10am–5.30pm. €6.

Reached via a narrow walkway and jutting into the river, the impressive **Torre de Belém** (Tower of Belém) has become an iconic symbol of Lisbon. It is fashioned in the Manueline style that was prominent during the reign of Manuel, its windows and stairways embellished with arches and decorative symbols representing Portugal's explorations into the New World. Built as a fortress to defend the mouth of the River Tejo, it took five years to complete, though when it opened in 1520 it would have been near the centre of the river – the earthquake of 1755 shifted the river's course. Today, visitors are free to explore the tower's various levels, which include a terrace facing the river from where artillery would have been fired. You can then climb a very steep spiral staircase up four levels – each with a slightly different framed view of the river – to a top terrace where you get a blowy panorama of Belém. You can also duck into the dungeons, a low-ceilinged room used to store gunpowder; these were also used notoriously by Dom Miguel to lock up political prisoners in the nineteenth century.

Museu dos Coches

MAP P.84, POCKET MAP D4
Avda Índia 136 and Praça Afonso de Albuquerque ☎ 210 732 319, ⓦ museudoscoches.pt. Tues–Sun 10am–6pm. Museu dos Coches €8, Royal Riding School €4, both €10, free Sun am.
Housed in a vast contemporary building, the **Museu dos Coches** (Coach Museum) contains one of the world's largest collections of carriages and saddlery, including a rare sixteenth-century coach designed for King Felipe I. Heavily gilded, ornate and often beautifully painted, the royal carriages, sedan chairs and children's cabriolets dating from the sixteenth to nineteenth centuries, contrast with the stark modern building, which gives great views over Belém and the river. More coaches from the collection are on display in the former Royal Riding School across the road, though it's only really the historic building itself that warrants the additional entrance fee.

MAAT

MAP P.84, POCKET MAP D4
Avda de Brasília ☎ 210 028 130, ⓦ www. maat.pt. Mon & Wed–Sun 11am–7pm. €9, free first Sun of the month.
British architect Amanda Levete has designed a sumptuous modern building on the riverfront to house the innovative **MAAT** (Museum of Art, Architecture and Technology). It's connected to the former Museu da Electricidade next door, a disused red-brick, early-twentieth-century power station, to give eight galleries of exhibition space dedicated to contemporary designers, artists and architects. Regularly changing exhibits feature the likes of Charles and Ray Eames and French artist Dominique Gonzalez-Foerster, while the permanent art collection showcases works by around 250 contemporary Portuguese artists. There are plans to hold film screenings, too. But as interesting as the exhibits can be, it is the striking building that's really

MAAT

captured people's imagination; a fluid, curving structure covered in 15,000 ceramic tiles that seems to glow at sunset. The galleries (including the giant Oval Room for the show-stopping exhibits) are sunk below street level, which means you can easily walk up onto the cantilevered roof for wonderful views across the river.

Palácio da Ajuda

MAP P.84, POCKET MAP D2
Largo da Ajuda. Tram #18 from Praça do Comércio or bus #729 from Belém ☎ 213 620 264, ⓦ palacioajuda.pt. Mon, Tues & Thurs–Sun 10am–6pm. €5, free first Sun of the month.

This massive **nineteenth-century palace** sits on a hillside above Belém. Construction began in 1802, but was left incomplete when João VI and the royal family fled to Brazil to escape Napoleon's invading army in 1807. The original plans were therefore never fulfilled, though the completed section was used as a royal residence after João returned from exile in 1821. The crashingly tasteless decor was commissioned by the nineteenth-century royal, Dona Maria II (João's granddaughter), and gives an insight into the opulent life the royals lived. The Queen's bedroom comes complete with a polar bear-skin rug, while the throne and ballroom are impressive for their sheer size and extravagance. The highly ornate banqueting hall, full of crystal chandeliers, is also breathtaking, while the recently renovated West Wing houses the Royal Treasury.

Jardim Botânico da Ajuda

MAP P.84, POCKET MAP C2
Entrance on Calçada da Ajuda and Calçada do Galvão ☎ 213 622 503, ⓦ isa.ulisboa. pt. Daily: May–Sept 10am–6pm; Oct–April 10am–5pm. €2.

A classic example of formal Portuguese gardening, this is one of the city's oldest and most interesting **botanical gardens**. Commissioned by the Marquês de Pombal and laid out in 1768, it was owned by the royal family until the birth of the Republic in 1910, then restored in the 1990s. The garden is split into eight parts planted with species from around the world, arranged around terraces, statues and fountains, much of it with lovely river views.

Páteo Alfacinha

MAP P.84, POCKET MAP D2
Rua do Guarda Jóias 44 ☎ 213 628 258, ⓦ pateoalfacinha.com.

Just five minutes' walk from the Palácio da Ajuda, it is worth seeking out this highly picturesque *páteo* – a renovated cluster of traditional nineteenth-century Lisbon houses gathered round a central patio. These were common in the days when families lived in tight-knit communities who looked after and traded with each other. Today the houses only come alive for special events and private parties, often at weekends, though there are two decent restaurants (closed Sundays), one which is open in summer and the other in winter.

Parque Florestal de Monsanto

MAP P.84, POCKET MAP E2
Bus #729 from Ajuda or Belém.

The extensive hillside **Parque Florestal de Monsanto** – home to the city's main and well-equipped campsite (ⓦ lisboacamping.com) – is known as "Lisbon's lungs" though it used to be infamous for the prostitutes who worked here until the Mayor of Lisbon bought a house nearby in 2003. Suddenly the park was given a new lease of life and the hookers have been replaced by horse-and-trap rides to its splendid viewpoints. At weekends in summer the area is completely traffic-free and pop concerts are often laid on, usually free of charge.

Restaurants

Floresta de Belém

MAP P.84, POCKET MAP C4
Praça Afonso de Albuquerque 1a
☎ 213 636 307, ⓦ florestadebelem.com.
Tues–Sat noon–5pm & 7pm–11pm, Sun
noon–5pm.

On the corner with Rua Vieira
Portuense, this attracts a largely
Portuguese clientele, especially for
lunch at the weekend. Great salads,
grills and fresh fish from around
€7–9, served inside or on a sunny
outdoor terrace.

Portugália

MAP P.84, POCKET MAP C4
Avda de Brasilia Edif. Espelho d'Água
☎ 213 032 700, ⓦ portugalia.pt. Daily
noon–midnight.

Marooned on a little island in
an artificial lake facing the
Padrão dos Descobrimentos,
this glass-fronted restaurant has
a serene position. Dishes include
bitoques (small steaks) from €11
and a wonderful *gambas à brás*
(prawns with stick potatoes and
onions). Most mains €12–€16.

Solar do Embaixador

MAP P.84, POCKET MAP D4
Rua do Embaixador 210–212
☎ 213 625 111. Mon & Wed–Sun
12.30–3pm & 7–10.30pm.

Close to the Coach Museum,
this homely restaurant serves
favourites such as *bitoque* (thin
steak), *alheira* sausages and fresh
fish from €7–9, plus Brazilian
dishes such as *moqueca de peixe*
(fish stew; €19).

Café

Pastéis de Belém

MAP P.84, POCKET MAP C4
Rua de Belém 84–92 ⓦ pasteisdebelem.
pt. Daily 8am–midnight, Oct–May
closes 11pm.

No visit to Belém is complete
without a coffee and hot *pastel*

Pastéis de Belém

de nata (Portuguese egg tart)
liberally sprinkled with *canela*
(cinnamon) in this cavernous,
tiled pastry shop and café –
something of an institution
since it began serving them up
in 1837. The place positively
heaves, especially at weekends,
so expect a wait, although there's
usually space to sit down in its
warren of rooms.

Bar

À Margem

MAP P.84, POCKET MAP B5
Doca do Bom Sucesso ☎ 918 620 032,
ⓦ amargem.com. Mon–Thurs & Sun
10am–10pm, Fri & Sat 10am–1am.

Chic and minimalist café-bar with
stunning views across the river –
tables spill out onto the waterfront.
Sarnies from €7, plus tapas, salads
and a good list of cocktails and
wines. It's near the brick-striped
stumpy lighthouse.

Avenida, Parque Eduardo VII and the Gulbenkian

Lisbon's main avenue, Avenida da Liberdade (simply known as "Avenida"), links the centre with Parque Eduardo VII, best known for its views and enormous hothouses. The avenue, together with its side streets, was once home to statesmen and public figures. On its western side is the historic Praça das Amoreiras, the finishing point of the massive Águas Livres aqueduct. Here you'll find the Árpád Szenes-Vieira da Silva Foundation, a collection of works by two artists heavily influenced by Lisbon. Northwest of the park, the Fundação Calouste Gulbenkian is undoubtedly Portugal's premier cultural centre, featuring one of Europe's richest art collections. Art-lovers have a further attraction to the east, where you can view the historic paintings and objects in the Casa Museu Dr Anastácio Gonçalves. Just north of here is the bullring at Campo Pequeno, while east lies the city's zoo.

Avenida da Liberdade

MAP P.92, POCKET MAP J5

The 1.3km, palm-lined **Avenida da Liberdade** is still much as poet Fernando Pessoa described it: "the finest artery in Lisbon… full of trees… small gardens, ponds, fountains, cascades and statues". It was laid out in 1882 as the city's main north–south avenue and has several appealing outdoor cafés beneath the shade of trees that help cushion the roar of traffic. Some of the original nineteenth-century mansions remain, though most have been replaced by modern buildings. The upper end of the avenue (Lisbon's most expensive real estate) houses many of the city's designer shops and ends in a swirl of traffic at the landmark roundabout of Praça Marquês de Pombal (Rotunda).

Parque Mayer

MAP P.92, POCKET MAP J5

Opened in 1922 as an "entertainment precinct" when theatres were all the rage, the run-down **Parque Mayer** is still home to the Teatro Maria Vitória. The latest of many plans for redevelopment may see the site turned into a Cultural Village, complete with a School of Dance, Toy Museum and cinema, and the possible renovation of the **Teatro Capitólio**, Portugal's first great Modernist structure.

Casa-Museu Medeiros e Almeida

MAP P.92, POCKET MAP H5

Rua Rosa Araújo 41 ☎ 213 547 892, Ⓦ casa-museumedeirosealmeida.pt. Mon–Sat 10am–5pm. €5, free Sat 10am–1pm.

This excellent **museum** was the home of the industrialist, philanthropist and art collector **António Medeiros** until his death in 1986. Today it serves as a showcase for his priceless series of artefacts. His collection of 225 Chinese porcelain items (some 2000 years old), sixteenth- to nineteenth-century watches, and English and Portuguese silverware is considered the most valuable in the world. Other highlights include glorious eighteenth-century *azulejos* in the Sala de Lago, a room complete with large water fountains; and a rare seventeenth-century clock, made for Queen Catherine of Bragança and mentioned by Samuel Pepys in his diary.

Praça das Amoreiras

MAP P.92, POCKET MAP G5

One of Lisbon's most tranquil squares, **Praça das Amoreiras** – complete with kids' play area – is dominated on its western side by the Águas Livres aqueduct (see page 94), with a chapel wedged into its arches.

On the south side the Mãe d'Água cistern (☎ 218 100 215; Tues–Sun 10am–12.30pm & 1.30–5.30pm; €3) marks the end of the line for the aqueduct. Built between 1746 and 1834, the castellated stone building contains a reservoir that once supplied

the city. The structure nowadays hosts occasional temporary art exhibitions. Head to the back where there are stairs leading on to the roof for great views over the city. Back on the square, the little kiosk café is a popular spot for a coffee or beer and also hosts occasional art exhibits.

Árpád Szenes-Vieira da Silva Foundation

MAP P.92, POCKET MAP G5
Praça das Amoreiras 56–58 ☎ 213 880 044, ⓦ fasvs.pt. Tues–Sun 10am–6pm. €5.
Árpád Szenes-Vieira da Silva Foundation is a small but highly appealing gallery dedicated to the works of two painters and the artists who have been influenced by them. Arpad Szenes (1897–1985) was a Hungarian-born artist and friend of Henri Matisse and Pierre Bonnard, among others. While in Paris in 1928 he met the Portuguese artist Maria Helena Vieira da Silva (1908–92), whose work was influenced by the surrealism of Joan Miró and Max Ernst, with both of whom

Mãe d'Água cistern, Praça das Amoreiras

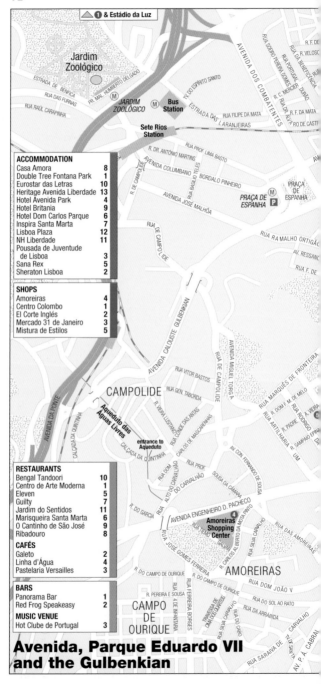

ACCOMMODATION

Casa Amora	8
Double Tree Fontana Park	1
Eurostar das Letras	10
Heritage Avenida Liberdade	13
Hotel Avenida Park	4
Hotel Britania	9
Hotel Dom Carlos Parque	6
Inspira Santa Marta	7
Lisboa Plaza	12
NH Liberdade	11
Pousada de Juventude de Lisboa	3
Sana Rex	5
Sheraton Lisboa	2

SHOPS

Amoreiras	4
Centro Colombo	1
El Corte Inglés	2
Mercado 31 de Janeiro	3
Mistura de Estilos	5

RESTAURANTS

Bengal Tandoori	10
Centro de Arte Moderna	1
Eleven	5
Guilty	7
Jardim do Sentidos	11
Marisqueira Santa Marta	6
O Cantinho de São José	9
Ribadouro	8

CAFÉS

Galeto	2
Linha d'Água	4
Pastelaria Versailles	3

BARS

Panorama Bar	1
Red Frog Speakeasy	2

MUSIC VENUE

Hot Clube de Portugal	3

Avenida, Parque Eduardo VII and the Gulbenkian

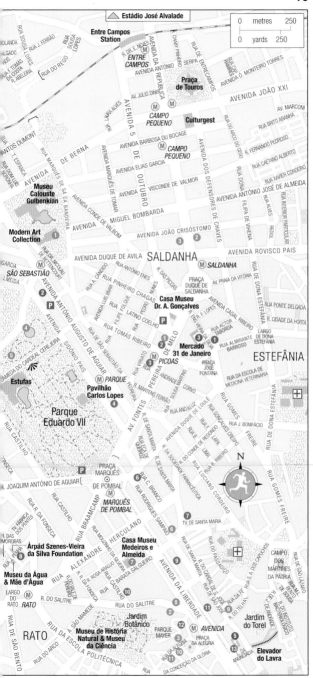

she was good friends. Szenes and Vieira da Silva married in 1930 and, in 1936, both exhibited in Lisbon, where they briefly lived, before eventually settling in France. The foundation shows the development of the artists' works, with Vieira da Silva's more abstract, subdued paintings contrasting with flamboyant Szenes, some of whose paintings show the clear influence of Miró.

Aqueduto das Águas Livres

MAP P.92, POCKET MAP F4

Entrance on Calçada da Quintinha 6. Bus #712/#758 from Amoreiras ☏ 218 100 215. Tues–Sat 10am–5.30pm. €3.

The towering **Aqueduto das Águas Livres** was opened in 1748, bringing a reliable source of safe drinking water to the city for the first time. Stretching for 60km (most of it underground), the aqueduct stood firm during the 1755 earthquake, though it later gained a more notorious reputation thanks to one Diogo Alves, a nineteenth-century serial killer who threw his victims off the top – a seventy-metre drop. It is possible to walk across a 1.5km section of the aqueduct, though you'll need a head for heights. The walkable section is accessed off a quiet residential street through a small park in Campolide, 1km north of Praça das Amoreiras.

Fundação Calouste Gulbenkian

MAP P.92, POCKET MAP H2

Avda de Berna 45a ☏ 217 823 000, ⓦ gulbenkian.pt.

Set in extensive grounds, the **Fundação Calouste Gulbenkian** was set up by the Armenian oil magnate Calouste Gulbenkian (see page 94) whose legendary art-market coups included the acquisition of works from the Hermitage in St Petersburg. Today the Gulbenkian Foundation has a multi-million-dollar budget sufficient to finance work in all spheres of Portuguese cultural life. In this low-rise 1960s complex alone, it runs an orchestra, three concert halls and an attractive open-air amphitheatre.

Museu Calouste Gulbenkian: Founder's Collection

MAP P.92, POCKET MAP H2

Avda de Berna 45a ☏ 217 823 000, ⓦ gulbenkian.pt. Mon & Wed–Sun 10am–6pm. Combined ticket with Modern Art Collection €10, free Sun 2–6pm.

The **Museu Calouste Gulbenkian** combines the Founder's Collection

Calouste Gulbenkian

Calouste Sarkis Gulbenkian (1869–1955) was the Roman Abramovich of his era, making his millions from oil but investing in the world's best art rather than footballers. Born of wealthy Armenian parents in Istanbul in 1869, he followed his father into the oil industry and eventually moved to England. After the Russian Revolution of 1917 he bought works from the Leningrad Hermitage. During World War II, his Turkish background made him unwelcome in Britain and Gulbenkian auctioned himself to whoever would have him. Portugal bid an aristocratic palace (a marquês was asked to move out) and tax exemption, to acquire one of the most important cultural patrons of the century. From 1942 to his death in 1955, he accumulated one of the best private art collections in the world. His dying wish was that all of his collection should be displayed in one place, and this was granted in 1969 with the opening of the Museu Calouste Gulbenkian.

Lalique jewellry, Museu Calouste Gulbenkian

and the Modern Collection (see below). The **Founder's Collection** covers virtually every phase of Eastern and Western art. The small Egyptian room displays art from the Old Kingdom (c.2700 BC) up to the Roman period. Fine Roman statues, silver and glass, and gold jewellery from ancient Greece follow. The Islamic arts are magnificently represented by a variety of ornamental texts, opulently woven carpets, glassware and Turkish tiles. There is also porcelain from China, along with beautiful Japanese prints and lacquerwork.

European art includes work from all the major schools. The seventeenth-century collection yields Peter Paul Rubens' graphic *The Love of the Centaurs* (1635) and Rembrandt's *Figure of an Old Man*. Featured eighteenth-century works include those by Jean-Honoré Fragonard and Thomas Gainsborough – in particular the stunning *Portrait of Mrs Lowndes-Stone*. The big names of nineteenth- to twentieth-century France – Manet, Monet, Degas, Millet and Renoir – are all represented, along with John Sargent and Turner's vivid *Wreck of a Transport Ship* (1810). Elsewhere you'll find Sèvres porcelain and furniture from the reigns of Louis XV and Louis XVI. The last room features an amazing collection of Art Nouveau jewellery by René Lalique. Don't miss the fantastical *Peitoral-libélula* (Dragonfly breastpiece) brooch, decorated with enamelwork, gold and diamonds.

Museu Calouste Gulbenkian: Modern Collection

MAP P.92, POCKET MAP H2
Main entrance on Rua Dr Nicolau de Bettencourt ☎ 217 823 474, ⓦ gulbenkian. pt. Mon & Wed–Sun 10am–6pm. Combined ticket with Founders Collection €10, free Sun 2–6pm.

The **Modern Collection**, part of the Gulbenkian foundation (see above), features pop art, installations and sculptures – some witty, some baffling, but all thought-provoking. Most of the big names on the twentieth-century Portuguese scene are included, including portraits and sketches by José de Almada Negreiros (1873–1970), the founder of modernismo; the bright Futurist colours of Amadeo de Souza Cardoso; and artworks by Paula Rego, one of Portugal's leading contemporary artists, whose *Mãe* (1997) is outstanding. Pieces from major international artists such as David Hockney and Antony Gormley also feature in the collection.

Parque Eduardo VII

MAP P.92, POCKET MAP H4

The steep, formally laid out **Parque Eduardo VII** was named to honour Britain's King Edward VII when he visited the city in 1903. Its main building is the ornately tiled Pavilhão Carlos Lopes, built for the International Exhibition of Rio de Janeiro in 1922, then dismantled and rebuilt here in 1932; today, its hosts events and exhibitions such as the annual Moda Lisboa fashion week. North of here is the main viewing platform which offers commanding vistas of the city as well as Ferris wheel during the summer months. Another highlight

if you have children is the superb Parque Infantil (open daily; free), an inviting play area built round a mock galleon.

Two huge, rambling **estufas** (daily: April–Sept 10am–7pm; Oct–March 9am–5pm; €3.10, free Sun until 2pm; ⓦestufafria. cm-lisboa.pt) lie close by. Set in substantial former basalt quarries, both are filled with tropical plants, pools and endless varieties of palm and cactus. Of the two, the Estufa Quente (the hothouse) has the more exotic plants; the Estufa Fria (the coldhouse) hosts concerts and exhibitions.

Finally, the hilly northern reaches of the park contain an olive grove and a shallow lake which kids splash about in during the heat of the day.

Casa-Museu Dr Anastácio Gonçalves

MAP P.92, POCKET MAP J3

Avda 5 de Outubro 6–8. Entrance on Rua Pinheiro Chagas ⓘ213 540 823, ⓦpatrimoniocultural.gov.pt. Tues–Sat 10am–1pm & 2–6pm, Sun 10am–2pm & 3–6pm. €3.

This appealing neo-Romantic building with Art Nouveau

Parque Eduardo VII

Ethnic Lisbon

In the fifteenth century hundreds of Africans came to Lisbon on slave ships during Portugal's ruthless maritime explorations. Today, over 120,000 people of African and Asian descent live in the Greater Lisbon area, most hailing originally from Portugal's former colonies – Cape Verde, Angola, Mozambique, Brazil, Goa and Macao. The 1974 revolution and subsequent independence of the former colonies saw another wave of immigrants settle in the capital. Nowadays African and Brazilian culture permeates Lisbon life, influencing its music, food, television and street slang. Most Lisboetas are rightly proud of their cosmopolitan city, although, inevitably, racism persists and few from ethnic minorities have managed to break through the glass ceiling to the top jobs.

touches – including a beautiful stained-glass window – was originally built for painter José Malhoa in 1904, but now holds the exquisite **private collection** of ophthalmologist Dr Anastácio Gonçalves, who bought the house in the 1930s. Highlights include paintings by Portuguese landscape artist João Vaz and by Malhoa himself, who specialized in historical paintings – his *Dream of Infante Henriques* is a typical example. You'll also find Chinese porcelain from the sixteenth-century Ming dynasty, along with furniture from England, France, Holland and Spain dating from the seventeenth century.

Praça de Touros

MAP P.92, POCKET MAP J1
Campo Pequeno ☏ 217 998 450,
🖳 www.campopequeno.com.
Built in 1892, and substantially renovated in 2000 – with a retractable roof – the **Praça de Touros** at Campo Pequeno is an impressive Moorish-style bullring seating nine thousand spectators. The Portuguese *tourada* (bullfight) is not as famous as its Spanish counterpart, but as a spectacle it's marginally preferable, as here the bull isn't killed in the ring, but instead is wrestled to the ground in a genuinely elegant, colourful and skilled display. During the fight,

however, the bull is usually injured and slaughtered later in any case. Performances start at around 10pm on Thursday evenings from Easter to September. At other times, you can visit a small museum which details the history of the arena which you can also visit as part of a tour (10am–1pm & 2–6pm, 7pm in summer; €5, arena visit only €3). Surrounded by a ring of lively cafés and restaurants, the bullring also hosts concerts, live acts, musicals and other events. Beneath the arena is a surprisingly large underground shopping and cinema complex and a parking lot.

Jardim Zoológico

MAP P.92, POCKET MAP E1
Praça Marechal Humberto Delgado ☏ 217 232 900, 🖳 www.zoo.pt. Daily: March–Sept 10am–8pm; Oct–Feb 10am–6pm. €21.50, children under 12 €14.50.
Lisbon's **Jardim Zoológico** was opened in 1884 and makes for an enjoyable excursion. There's a café-lined park area which you can visit for free and see monkeys, crocodiles and parrots. Once inside the zoo proper, a small cable car (daily from 11am until 30min before closing; included in the price) transports you over many of the animals, and there's a well-stocked reptile house and feeding sessions for sea lions and pelicans. Just by its main gates lies

Jardim Zoológico

the Animax amusement park (daily 11am–7pm), where kids can load up a card for rides and games.

Estádio da Luz

MAP P.92

☎ 707 200 100, ⊕ slbenfica.pt.

One of the most famous stadia in the world, the **Estádio da Luz** was built for and hosted the final of Euro 2004, when Portugal lost in a shock defeat to Greece. This is the home to Benfica (officially called Sport Lisboa e Benfica), the giant of Portuguese football who win (together with Porto) most domestic trophies. It's usually easy to buy match tickets from the stadium ticket office (from €25–50): expect to see the club mascot eagle flying across the pitch before the game starts. There is also an impressive museum (☎217 219 500; daily 10am–6pm, match days until kick-off; €10 or €17.50 with stadium tour) with interactive exhibits tracing the club's prestigious history, including its two European Cup wins (1961 and 1962) and Europa League finals in 2013 and 2014.

Estádio José Alvalade

MAP P.92

Rua Professor Fernando da Fonseca, Apartado 4120 ☎ 217 516 000, ⊕ sporting. pt. Ticket office open Mon–Fri 10am–8pm, and match days 10am–start of second half.

The impressive **José Alvalade Stadium** is home to Sporting Clube de Portugal, better known as Sporting Lisbon. Seating over 50,000 spectators, the stadium was built for Euro 2004 adjacent to the original stadium. The team usually play second fiddle to city rivals Benfica (see above), but still boast an impressive array of trophies: over 18 league wins, 16 Portuguese Cup wins and a European Cup Winners Cup in 1964. Tickets for games (from €20–45) are available at the stadium ticket office. You can also take a tour of the stadium and visit the museum (Tues–Sun museum 11am–6pm; tours at 11am, 2.30pm, 3.30pm & 4.30pm; €14; ☎ 217 516 164), which features the shirt of one of the club's best known sons, Cristiano Ronaldo.

Shops

Amoreiras

MAP P.92, POCKET MAP F4
Avda Engenheiro Duarte Pacheco 2037. Bus
#758 from Cais de Sodré Ⓦ amoreiras.com.
Daily 10am–11pm.

Amoreiras, Lisbon's striking,
postmodern commercial centre,
is a wild fantasy of pink and blue
towers sheltering ten cinemas, sixty
cafés and restaurants, 250 shops,
a hotel and a roof terrace with
panoramic views over the city (€5).
Built in 1985 and designed by
adventurous Portuguese architect
Tomás Taveira, most of its stores
are open daily; Sunday sees the
heaviest human traffic, with
entire families descending for an
afternoon out.

Centro Colombo

MAP P.92, POCKET MAP F1
Avda Lusíada Ⓜ Colégio Militar/Luz,
Ⓦ colombo.pt. Most shops daily 10am–
midnight.

Iberia's largest shopping centre
is almost a town in its own
right, with over 340 shops,
65 restaurants and ten cinema
screens. Major stores include Fnac,
Timberland, Sports Zone and Toys
"R" Us, while the top floor has
the usual fast-food outlets along
with a sit-down dining area in the
jungle-themed "Cidade Perdida"
(Lost City).

El Corte Inglés

MAP P.92, POCKET MAP H3
Avda António Augusto de Aguiar 31
Ⓦ elcorteingles.pt. Most shops Mon–Sat
10am–10pm, Sun 10am–8pm. Cinema info
on Ⓦ ucicinemas.pt.

A giant Spanish department store
spread over nine floors, two of
which are underground. The
basement specializes in gourmet
food, with various delis, bakers
and a supermarket (closed Sun
afternoon), while the upper floors
offer a range of stylish goods,
including clothes, sports gear,
books, CDs and toys. The top
floor packs in cafés and restaurants.
There's also a fourteen-screen
cinema in the basement.

Mercado 31 de Janeiro

MAP P.92, POCKET MAP J3
Rua Enginheiro Viera da Silva ☎ 218 160
970. Tues–Sat 7am–2pm.

This bustling local market is
divided into sections; you'll find
a colourful array of fresh fruit,
vegetables, spices, fish, flowers and
a few crafts.

Mistura de Estilos

MAP P.92, POCKET MAP J5
Rua São José 21. Mon–Fri 4–9pm (7pm
in winter).

This tiny shop sells individually
crafted tiles from around €4 – as
the name implies, the styles are
mixed – from plain patterns to
lovely animal motifs – but most are
simple, effective and portable.

Restaurants

Bengal Tandoori

MAP P.92, POCKET MAP J5
Rua da Alegria 23 ☎ 213 479 918,
Ⓦ bengal.pt. Daily noon–midnight.

The decor might be Greco-Roman,
but this is rated as one of the best
Indian restaurants in town, up a
steep side-street. Expect all the
usual dishes – madras, biryanis and,
of course, excellent tandoori – in an
intimate space with good service.
Mains from €8–16.

Centro de Arte Moderna

MAP P.92, POCKET MAP H2
Rua Dr Bettencourt, Fundação Calouste
Gulbenkian ☎ 217 822 751. Mon & Wed–
Sun 10am–6pm.

Join the lunchtime queues at the
museum restaurant for bargain
hot and cold dishes. There's an
excellent choice of salads for
vegetarians. Similar food is offered
in the basement of the Gulbenkian
museum, with outdoor seats facing
the gardens.

Eleven

Eleven

MAP P.92, POCKET MAP G3
Rua Marquês da Fronteira ☎ 213 862
211, ⓦ restauranteleven.com. Mon–Sat
12.30–3pm & 7.30–11pm.

At the top of Parque Eduardo VII,
this Michelin-starred restaurant,
under the watchful eye of German
head chef Joachim Koerper, hits
the heights both literally and
metaphorically. The interior is
both intimate and bright, with
wonderful city views. The food is
expensive but not outrageous, with
mains around €40–50 or a tasting
menu at €95. Dishes include sea
bass with chestnuts or suckling pig
with passion fruit, and there's a
fine wine list.

Guilty

MAP P.92, POCKET MAP H5
Rua Barata Salgueiro 28 ☎ 211 913 590,
ⓦ guilty.olivier.pt. Tues–Sun 12.30–3.30pm
& 7.30pm–midnight, bar open Thurs–Sat
until 4am.

Classy comfort foods are served
(hence the name) in this modern
diner, including pasta, carpaccio,
giant pizzas and gourmet burgers
(mains €11–17) from renowned
chef Olivier. Just off the Avenida da
Liberdade, it's a fashionable spot,
too, with nighttime DJs.

Jardim do Sentidos

MAP P.92, POCKET MAP J5
Rua Mãe d'Água 3 ☎ 213 423 670.
Mon–Sat noon–3pm & 7–10.30pm.

This attractive, long space opens
onto a pleasant garden. The food
is vegetarian and vegan, with
set buffet lunches (around €11)
featuring the likes of *tofu á bras* and
evening mains such as couscous
and lasagne.

Marisqueira Santa Marta

MAP P.92, POCKET MAP J4
Trav do Enviato de Inglaterra 1 (off Rua
de Santa Marta) ☎ 213 525 638. Daily
noon–midnight.

Attractive and spacious *marisqueira*
with bubbling tanks of crabs
in one corner. Service is very
attentive and meals end with a
complimentary port, after which
you don't usually care that the bill
is slightly above average (mains
from €12).

O Cantinho de São José

MAP P.92, POCKET MAP J5
Rua São José 94 ☎ 213 427 866.
Mon–Fri & Sun 11am–11pm.

Friendly *tasca* serving good-value
food – tuck into a full meal of
grilled meat, salmon or other fish
with wine, and you may get change
from €15.

Ribadouro

MAP P.92, POCKET MAP J5
Avda da Liberdade 155 ☎ 213 549 411,
ⓦ cervejariaribadouro.pt. Daily noon–1am.

The Avenida's best *cervejaria*,
serving excellent seafood,
including the superb speciality
prawns with garlic (around €18)
and pricier lobster, crab, oysters
and clams – they also do a decent
bacalhão (salted cod) for €13. If
you don't fancy a full meal, take

a seat at the bar and order a beer with a plate of prawns. It's best to book for the restaurant, especially at weekends.

Cafés

Galeto

MAP P.92, POCKET MAP J2
Avda da República 14 ☎ 213 544 444. Daily 7am–3am.
Late-opening café with striking 1960s decor and an array of snacks, pastries, beers and coffees. Drop in for a full meal at sensible prices by the bar.

Linha d'Água

MAP P.92, POCKET MAP G3
Jardim Amália Rodrigues ☎ 213 814 327. Daily 10am–midnight; Oct–March closes 8pm.
Facing a small lake, this glass-fronted café is at the northern end of the park. It's a tranquil spot to sip a coffee or beer, and decent buffet lunches are served, too.

Pastelaria Versailles

MAP P.92, POCKET MAP J2
Avda da República 15a ☎ 213 546 340. Daily 7.30am–11.45pm.
This lovely traditional café, full of bustling waiters, is busiest at around 4pm, when Lisbon's elderly dames gather for a chat and a coffee beneath the statement chandeliers. The decor here is as charming at the pastries.

Bar

Panorama Bar

MAP P.92, POCKET MAP J3
Sheraton Lisboa, Rua Latino Coelho 1 ☎ 213 120 000. Daily 3pm–2am.
Stroll into this high-rise hotel and take the lift to the spectacular top-floor cocktail bar (open to the public). Drinks aren't cheap, but dubbed Lisbon's eighth hill, the bar commands the best views of the city.

Red Frog Speakeasy

MAP P.92, POCKET MAP J5
Rua do Salitre 5A ☎ 215 831 120. Mon–Sat 6pm–3am.
Taking inspiration from the prohibition era in the US, this upmarket cocktail bar has a secretive air, enhanced by the fact you have to ring a bell to enter (look for the red frog on the wall). Many of the best cocktails (from around €10) are made from local Portuguese brandies, *ginginha* and herbal liqueurs: try the Mr Brown, spiked with gin and Madeira wine and mixed with earl grey tea, rhubarb and bergamot.

Music venue

Hot Clube de Portugal

MAP P.92, POCKET MAP J5
Praça da Alegria 48 ☎ 213 619 740, ⓦ hcp.pt. Tues–Sat 10pm–2am.
Dating from 1948 – making it one of Europe's oldest jazz clubs – this tiny basement club hosts top names in the jazz world, along with a range of local performers. The venue was largely rebuilt after a recent fire.

Pastelaria Versailles

Parque das Nações

The Parque das Nações (pronounced "na-soysh"), or "Park of Nations", is the high-tech former site of Expo '98. Its flat, pedestrianized walkways, lined with fountains and futuristic buildings, are in complete contrast to the narrow, precipitous streets of old Lisbon, and it is packed with locals on summer weekends. The main highlight is the giant Oceanário de Lisboa, but it also features a casino, a cable car, riverside walkways, a giant park and two of Lisbon's largest concert venues. It is also impossible to miss the astonishing 17km-long Vasco da Gama bridge over the Tejo. Constructed in time for the Expo in 1998, it is still the longest bridge in Western Europe.

Olivais dock and the Altice Arena

MAP P.104, POCKET MAP B17–18

The central focus of the Parque das Nações is the Olivais dock, overlooked by pixie-hatted twin towers, and where boats pull in on Tejo cruises (see page 138). The dock's **Marina** (☎ 218 949 066) offers canoeing and sailing lessons and riverboat tours. The main building facing the dock is the Pavilhão de Portugal (Portugal Pavilion), a multipurpose arena designed by Álvaro Siza Vieira, architect of the reconstructed Chiado district, featuring an enormous, sagging concrete canopy on its south side. It now hosts temporary exhibitions. Opposite here – past Antony Gormley's weird *Rhizome* sculpture, a tree of cast-iron legs – is the spaceship-like **Altice Arena** (☎ 218 918 440, ⓦ arena.meo.pt), Portugal's largest indoor arena and the venue for major visiting bands (including Justin Bieber, Coldplay and Madonna) and sporting events. It also hosted the 2005 MTV Europe Music Awards and the Eurovision Song Contest 2018.

Pavilhão do Conhecimento (Ciência Viva)

MAP P.104, POCKET MAP B18
Alameda dos Oceanos ☎ 218 917 100, ⓦ pavconhecimento.pt. Tues–Fri 10am–6pm, Sat & Sun 11am–7pm. €9, children under 17 €7.
Run by Portugal's Ministry of Science and Technology, the

Visiting the park

The best way to reach the park is to take the metro to Oriente or bus #728 from Praça do Comércio. Oriente metro station exits in the bowels of the Estação do Oriente, a cavernous glass and concrete station designed by esteemed Spanish architect Santiago Calatrava.

The park's website (☎ 218 919 333, ⓦ portaldasnacoes.pt) has details of the day's events, and information about the urban art dotted round the area, from murals and graffiti art to statues and sculptures.

Waterfall of the Jardins da Água, Parque das Nações

Knowledge Pavilion (Live Science) hosts excellent changing exhibitions on subjects like 3D animation and the latest computer technology, and is usually bustling with school parties. The permanent interactive exhibits – allowing you to create a vortex in water or a film of detergent the size of a baby's blanket – are particularly good, and there's also a cybercafé with free internet.

Jardins da Água

MAP P.104, POCKET MAP B19

The **Jardins da Água** (Water Gardens), crisscrossed by waterways and ponds, are based on the stages of a river's drainage pattern, from stream to estuary. They are not huge, but linked by stepping stones, and there are enough gushing fountains, water gadgets and pumps to keep children occupied for hours.

Oceanário

MAP P.104, POCKET MAP B18
Esplanada Dom Carlos I ☏ 218 917 002, ⓦ oceanario.pt. Daily: May–Sept 10am–8pm; Oct–April 10am–7pm. €15, children under 12 €10, family ticket €39.
Designed by Peter Chermayeff and looking like something

off the set of a James Bond film, Lisbon's **Oceanário** (Oceanarium) is one of Europe's largest and contains some 8000 fish and marine animals. Its main feature is the enormous central tank which you can look into from different levels for close-up views of circling sharks down to the rays burying themselves in the sand. Almost more impressive, though, are the re-creations of various ocean ecosystems, such as the Antarctic tank, containing frolicking penguins, and the Pacific tank, where otters bob about in the rock pools. On a darkened lower level, smaller tanks contain shoals of brightly coloured tropical fish and other warm-water creatures. Find a window free of school parties and the whole experience becomes the closest you'll get to deep-sea diving without getting wet.

The Teleférico and the Jardins Garcia de Orta

MAP P.104, POCKET MAP B16–18
ⓦ telecabinelisboa.pt. Daily: June to mid-Sept 10.30am–8pm; mid-Sept to Oct & mid-March to May 11am–7pm; Nov

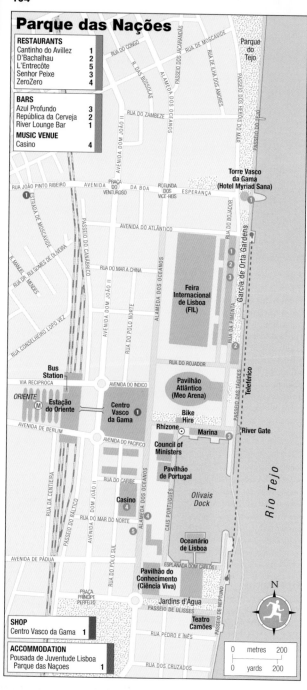

Parque das Nações

RESTAURANTS

Cantinho do Avillez	1
D'Bachalhau	2
L'Entrecôte	5
Senhor Peixe	3
ZeroZero	4

BARS

Azul Profundo	3
República da Cerveja	2
River Lounge Bar	1

MUSIC VENUE

Casino	4

SHOP

Centro Vasco da Gama 1

ACCOMMODATION

Pousada de Juventude Lisboa
Parque das Nações 1

Vasco da Gama

The opening of Parque das Nações in 1998 celebrated the 500th anniversary of Vasco da Gama's arrival in India. One of Portugal's greatest explorers, Da Gama was born in Sines in 1460. By the 1490s he was working for João II, protecting trading stations along the African coast. This persuaded the next king, Manuel I, to commission him to find a sea route to India. He departed Lisbon in July 1497 with a fleet of four ships, reaching southern Africa in December. The following May they finally reached Calicut in southwest India, obtaining trading terms before departing in August 1498. The return voyage took a full year, by which time Da Gama had lost two of his ships and half his men. But he was richly rewarded by the king, his voyage inspiring Camões to write *Os Lusiadas*, Portugal's most famous epic poem. Da Gama returned to India twice more, the final time in 1524 when he contracted malaria and died in the town of Cochin.

to mid-March 11am–6pm. €4 one-way, €6 return. Children under 12 €2 single, €3.50 return.

The ski-lift-style *teleférico* (cable car) rises up to 20m as it shuttles you over Olivais docks to the northern side of the Parque, giving commanding views over the site on the way. It drops down to the **Garcia de Orta gardens**, containing exotic trees from Portugal's former colonies. Behind the gardens, Rua Pimenta is lined with a motley collection of international restaurants, from Irish to Israeli.

Torre Vasco da Gama

MAP P.104, POCKET MAP B16
Cais das Naus ☎ 211 107 600,
ⓦ myriad.pt.

Once an integral part of an oil refinery, the **Torre Vasco da Gama** (Vasco da Gama Tower) is, at 145m high, Lisbon's tallest structure. The tower is now integrated into the five-star hotel *Myriad by Sana*, Lisbon's answer to Dubai's *Burj Al Arab*.

Parque do Tejo

MAP P.104, POCKET MAP B15
Unfurling along the waterfront for 2km right up to the Vasco da Gama bridge, **Parque do Tejo** is

threaded through with bike trails and riverside walks. It's also a great spot for a picnic – supplies are available in the Vasco da Gama shopping centre.

Feira Internacional de Lisboa

MAP P.104, POCKET MAP B16–17
Rua do Bojador ☎ 218 921 500,
ⓦ www.fil.pt.

Lisbon's trade fair hall, the **Feira Internacional de Lisboa** (FIL), hosts various events, including a handicrafts fair displaying ceramics and crafts from around the country (usually in July).

Torre Vasco da Gama

Shop

Centro Vasco da Gama

MAP P.104, POCKET MAP B17
Avda D. João II 40 ☎ 218 930 600,
Ⓦ centrovascodagama.pt. Daily 9am–
midnight.

Three floors of local and
international stores are housed
beneath a glass roof, washed
by permanently running water;
international branches include
Zara, Timberland, Swatch and
C&A, and local sports and
bookshops also feature. There
are plenty of fast-food outlets
and good-value restaurants
on the top floor, six cinema
screens, children's areas and a
Continente supermarket on the
lower floor.

Restaurants

Cantinho do Avillez

MAP P.104, POCKET MAP C13
Rua Bojador 55 ☎ 218 700 365,
Ⓦ cantinhodoavillez.pt. Mon–Fri noon–3pm
& 6–11pm, Sat & Sun noon–11pm.
The top place to eat in the
Parque das Nações, this bright
contemporary restaurant opens
onto a great outdoor terrace

and serves sublime food by
esteemed chef José Avillez. The
innovative menu features his
trademark Portuguese dishes with
a twist, such as cod served with
exploding olives, Algarvian shrimp
with Thai sauce and hamburger
with foie gras. Mains cost from
around €15.

D'Bacalhau

MAP P.104, POCKET MAP B16
Rua do Pimenta 43–45 ☎ 218 941 296,
Ⓦ restaurantebacalhau.com. Daily
noon–4pm & 7–11pm.
If you want to sample one of the
alleged 365 recipes for *bacalhau*
– salted cod – this is a good place
to come, as it serves quite a range
of them from €9: *bacalhau com
natas* (with a creamy sauce) is
particularly good. There are also
other dishes, including a selection
of fresh fish and meat dishes from
around €13.

L'Entrecôte

MAP P.104, POCKET MAP B18
Alameda dos Oceanos 1.02.12a ☎ 218 962
220. Daily 12.30–3pm & 7.30–11.30pm.
Local branch of the Lisbon
restaurant famed for its fabulous
steaks cooked with sublime sauces
– choose from various menus
starting at €10.

Cantinho do Avillez

Senhor Peixe

MAP P.104, POCKET MAP B16

Rua da Pimenta 35–37 ☏ 218 955 892.
Tues–Sat noon–3.30pm & 7–10.30pm,
Sun noon–3.30pm.

"Mr Fish" is widely thought to serve
up some of the best fresh seafood
in the Lisbon region – check the
counter for the day's catch or choose
a lobster from the bubbling tank.
Most dishes – from around €15
– are grilled in the open kitchen.
There's also a little fish-themed bar
and pleasant outdoor tables.

ZeroZero

MAP P.104, POCKET MAP B18

Alameda dos Oceanos, Lote 2 ☏ 218 957
016, ⓦ pizzeriazerozero.pt. Mon–Thurs &
Sun noon–midnight, Fri & Sat noon–1am.

This classy pizza restaurant uses
Italian ingredients for its tasty
pizzas (€9–15) and also serves a
range of pastas, salads and quality
antipasti. There's also a bar serving
prosecco and cocktails, plus an
outside terrace with river views.

Bars

Azul Profundo

MAP P.104, POCKET MAP B17

Rossio dos Olivais, Quiosque 4. Daily
10am–2am, closes 7pm from Oct–April.

Overlooking the glittering docks,
this sunny esplanade bar offers a
good range of snacks, fruit juices
and fantastic *caipirinha* cocktails
along with inexpensive lunches.

República da Cerveja

MAP P.104, POCKET MAP B17

Jardim das Tágides 2.26.01 ☏ 218 922 590.
Daily 12.30pm–1am, closes midnight from
Oct–Feb.

In a great position close to the
water's edge and facing the Vasco
da Gama bridge, this modern bar-
restaurant specializes in some fine
international beers, though sticking
to Super Bock will save a few euros.
Steaks, burgers and sausages are also
on offer (mains from €10–16), and
there's occasional live music.

Casino

River Lounge Bar

MAP P.104, POCKET MAP B16

Myriad by Sana, Cais das Naus, Lote
2.23.01 ☏ 211 107 600, ⓦ myriad.pt.
Daily noon–midnight.

Inside the deluxe *Myriad by
Sana* hotel, the ultra-hip *River
Lounge Bar* juts into the Tejo so
you feel as if you're right on the
water. Cocktails and drinks are
predictably expensive, but it's
worth it for the view. Frequent live
music after 7pm.

Music venue

Casino

MAP P.104, POCKET MAP A18

Alameda dos Oceanos 45 ☏ 218 929 000,
ⓦ casino-lisboa.pt. Mon–Thurs & Sun
3pm–3am, Fri & Sat 4pm–4am.

Opened in 2006, this state-of-the-
art space – with its glass-cylinder
entrance hall – hosts top shows
from Broadway and London
as well as major concerts in the
performance hall, which has a
retractable roof. The usual casino
attractions also feature.

Sintra

If you make just one day-trip from Lisbon, choose the beautiful hilltop town of Sintra, the former summer residence of Portuguese royalty and a UNESCO World Heritage Site since 1995. Not only does the town boast two of Portugal's most extraordinary palaces, it also contains a semitropical garden, a Moorish castle and proximity to some great beaches. Looping around a series of wooded ravines and with a climate that encourages moss and ferns to grow from every nook and cranny, Sintra consists of three districts: Sintra-Vila, with most of the historical attractions; Estefânia, a ten-minute walk to the east, where trains from Lisbon pull in; and São Pedro to the south, well known for its antique shops and best visited on the eve of São Pedro (June 28–29), the main saint's day, and for its market on the second and fourth Sunday of the month.

Sintra-Vila

MAP P.110

The historic centre of Sintra spreads across the slopes of several steep hills, themselves loomed over by wooded heights topped by the Moorish castle and the Palácio da Pena. Dominating the centre of **Sintra-Vila** are the tapering chimneys of the Palácio Nacional, surrounded by tall houses painted in pale pink, ochre or yellow, many with ornate turrets and balconies peering out to the plains of Lisbon

Palácio Nacional

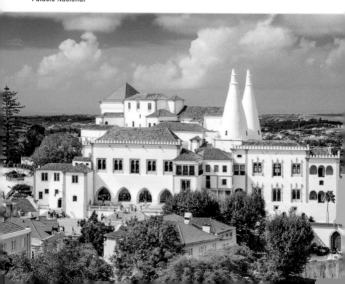

Visiting Sintra

There are trains from Lisbon's Rossio station (every 10–30min; 45min; €2.75 single). A land train (every 30min from 10.30am–dusk; €5 day-ticket) runs from Sintra station to São Pedro and back via Sintra-Vila. Alternatively, bus #434 takes a circular route from Sintra station to most of the sites mentioned in this chapter (every 20–40min from 9.30am–6.20pm; €5.50) and allows you to get on and off whenever you like on the circuit. Also useful is bus #435 which runs from Sintra station to Monserrate gardens via Sintra-Vila and Quinta da Regaleira (every 45min 9.40am–6.15pm; €5 return). To see the area around Sintra, including the coast, consider a Day-rover (Turístico Diário) ticket on the local Scotturb buses (Ⓦ scotturb.com; €15). Ask at the tourist office about various combined tickets that can save money on entry to the main sites.

far below. All this is highly scenic – though, in fact, Sintra looks at its best seen on the way in from the station. Summer crowds can swamp the narrow central streets, and once you've seen the sights, you're best off heading to the surrounding attractions up in the hills.

Palácio Nacional

MAP P.110
Largo da Rainha Dona Amélia
Ⓣ 219 106 840, Ⓦ parquesdesintra.pt.
Daily: March–Oct 9.30am–7pm; Nov–Feb 9.30am–5.30pm. €10.

Best seen early or late in the day to avoid the crowds, the sumptuous **Palácio Nacional** was probably already in existence at the time of the Moors. It takes its present form from the rebuilding of Dom João I (1385–1433) and his successor, Dom Manuel I, the chief royal beneficiary of Vasco da Gama's explorations. Its exterior style is an amalgam of Gothic – featuring impressive battlements – and Manueline, tempered inside by a good deal of Moorish influence. Sadly, after the fall of the monarchy in 1910, most of the surrounding walls and medieval houses were destroyed. Highlights on the lower floor include the Manueline **Sala dos Cisnes**, so-called for the swans (*cisnes*) on

its ceiling, and the Sala das Pegas, which takes its name from the flock of magpies (*pegas*) painted on the frieze and ceiling – João I, caught in the act of kissing a lady-in-waiting by his queen, reputedly had the room decorated with as many magpies as there were women at court, to imply they were all magpie-like gossips.

Best of the upper floor is the gallery above the palace chapel. Beyond, a succession of **state rooms** finishes with the Sala das Brasões, its domed and coffered ceiling emblazoned with the arms of 72 noble families. Finally, don't miss the kitchens, whose roofs taper into the giant chimneys that are the palace's distinguishing features. The Palace also hosts events for the Sintra Music Festival (see page 142).

MU.SA

MAP P.110
Avda Heliodoro Salgado Ⓣ 965 233 692,
Ⓦ cm-sintra.pt/musa-museu-das-artes-de-sintra. Tues–Fri 10am–6pm, Sat & Sun noon–6pm, summer open until 8pm. €1.

Inside Sintra's beautiful former casino, this appealing contemporary **art museum** is dedicated to important Portuguese artists such as Emílio de Paula Campos (1884–1943), who

SINTRA

Sintra

- Centro Cultural O. Cadaval
- MU.SA
- Market
- Câmara Municipal
- Train Station
- see Sintra-Vila
- SINTRA-VILA
- Quinta da Regaleira
- ESTEFÂNIA
- Parque da Liberdade
- Castelo dos Mouros
- Santa Maria
- SÃO PEDRO DE SINTRA
- São Pedro
- SANTA EUFÉMIA
- Ticket Office
- Ticket Office
- Palácio da Pena

| 0 | metres | 250 |
| 0 | yards | 250 |

Sintra-Vila

- Palácio Nacional
- LARGO RAINHA DONA AMÉLIA
- PRAÇA DA REPÚBLICA
- PRAÇA DA REPÚBLICA
- ESC. TEIXEIRA
- LARGO FERREIRA DE CASTRO

| 0 | metres | 50 |
| 0 | yards | 50 |

ACCOMMODATION

Casa do Valle	2
Chalet Relogio	6
Chalet Saudade	3
Hotel Nova Sintra	1
Hotel Sintra Jardim	5
Moon Hill Hostel	4

RESTAURANTS

A Tasca do Manel	3
Caldo Entornado	6
Cantinho de São Pedro	7
Incomum	2
Páteo do Garrett	11
Restaurante Regional de Sintra	1
Tulhas	10

CAFÉS

Adega das Caves	8
Casa Piriquita	9
Fábrica das Verdadeiras Queijadas da Sapa	5
Saudade	4

BARS

| Bar Fonte da Pipa | 2 |
| Café Paris | 1 |

portrays traditional rural scenes, and innovative sculptress Dorita Castel-Branco (1936–1996). There is also a photography room and temporary exhibits (fee payable).

Quinta da Regaleira

MAP P.110

Rua Barbosa do Bocage. ☎ 219 106 650, ⓦ regaleira.pt. Daily: Oct–March 9.30am–6pm; April–Sept 9.30am–8pm. Tours (90min) every 30–60min; advance booking essential. €12. Unguided visits €6.

The **Quinta da Regaleira** is one of Sintra's most elaborate estates. It was designed at the end of the nineteenth century by Italian architect and theatre set designer Luigi Manini for wealthy Brazilian merchant António Augusto Carvalho Monteiro. Manini's penchant for the dramatic is obvious: the principal building, the mock-Manueline **Palácio dos Milhões**, sprouts turrets and towers, while the interior boasts Art Nouveau tiles and elaborate Rococo wooden ceilings.

The surrounding **gardens** shelter fountains, terraces and grottoes, with the highlight being the Initiation Well, inspired by the initiation practices of the Freemasons. Entering via a Harry Potter-esque revolving stone door, you walk down a moss-covered spiral staircase to the foot of the well and through a tunnel, which eventually resurfaces at the edge of a lake (though in winter you exit from a shorter tunnel so as not to disturb a colony of hibernating bats).

In summer, the gardens host occasional performances of live music, usually classical or jazz.

Castelo dos Mouros

MAP P.110

☎ 219 237 300, ⓦ parquesdesintra.pt. Daily: March–Oct 9.30am–8pm; Nov–Feb 10am–6pm. €8.

Reached on bus #434, or a steep drive, the ruined ramparts of the **Castelo dos Mouros** are truly spectacular. It's also a pleasant, if steep, walk up (30–40min): start at the Calçada dos Clérigos, near the church of Santa Maria, where a stone pathway leads all the way up to the lower slopes, where you can see a Moorish grain silo and a ruined twelfth-century church. To enter the castle itself, you'll need

Castelo dos Mouros

Visiting Praia das Maçãs

Quaint old trams shuttle from near the Centro Cultural Olga Cadaval to the coastal resort of Praia das Maçãs via Colares (June–Sept 3–6pm daily; 50min; €3 single). However, check the latest routes and timetables on ☎ 219 238 766 or in the Sintra tourist office, as there are frequent shortenings of the route or alterations to the service.

to buy a ticket from the road exit. Built in the ninth century, the castle was taken from the Moors in 1147 by Afonso Henriques, Portugal's first monarch: the ruins of a Moorish mosque remain. The castle walls were allowed to fall into disrepair over subsequent centuries, though they were restored in the mid-nineteenth century under the orders of Ferdinand II. The castle is partly built into two craggy pinnacles, and views from up here are dazzling both inland and across to the Atlantic. Recent excavations have revealed the ruins of Muslim houses, thirty medieval Christian graves and ceramic vases dating back to the fifth century BC.

Palácio da Pena

Palácio da Pena

MAP P.110

Estrada da Pena ☎ 219 237 300,
Ⓦ parquedesintra.pt. Daily: March–Oct
9.45am–7pm; Nov–Feb 10am–6pm; last entry 1hr before closing. Palace and gardens €14, gardens only €7.50; reduced prices from Nov–Feb.

Bus #434 stops opposite the lower entrance to Parque da Pena, a stretch of rambling woodland with a scattering of lakes and follies. At the top of the park, about twenty minutes' walk from the entrance or a short ride on a shuttle bus (€3 return), looms the fabulous **Palácio da Pena**, a wild fantasy of domes, towers, ramparts and walkways, approached through

mock-Manueline gateways and a drawbridge that does not draw. A compelling riot of kitsch, the palace was built in the 1840s to the specifications of Ferdinand of Saxe-Coburg-Gotha, husband of Queen Maria II, with the help of the German architect Baron Eschwege. The interior is preserved exactly as it was left by the royal family when they fled Portugal in 1910. The result is fascinating: rooms of stone decorated to look like wood, statues of turbaned Moors nonchalantly holding electric chandeliers – it's all here. Of an original convent, founded in the early sixteenth century to celebrate the first sight of Vasco da Gama's returning fleet, only a beautiful, tiled chapel and Manueline cloister have been retained.

You can also look round the mock-Alpine **Chalet Condessa d'Edla** (€9.50, includes entry to park), built by Ferdinand in the 1860s as a retreat for his second wife.

Monserrate

MAP P.110

Estrada da Monserrate ⓘ 219 237 300, Ⓦ parquedesintra.pt Daily: March–Oct 9.30am–8pm; Nov–Feb 10am–5pm. €8.

The name most associated with the fabulous gardens and palace of **Monserrate** is that of William Beckford, the wealthiest untitled Englishman of his age, who rented the estate from 1793 to 1799, having been forced to flee Britain after he was caught in a compromising position with a sixteen-year-old boy. Setting about improving the place, he landscaped a waterfall and even imported a flock of sheep from his estate.

Half a century later, a second immensely rich Englishman, Sir Francis Cook, bought the estate and imported the head gardener from Kew to lay out water plants, tropical ferns and palms, and just about every known conifer. For a time Monserrate boasted the only

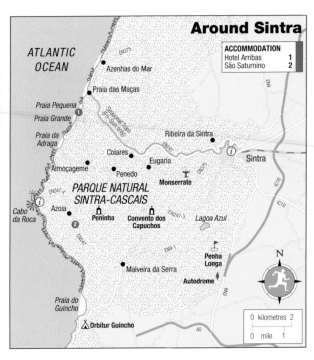

Around Sintra

ATLANTIC OCEAN

ACCOMMODATION
Hotel Arribas	1
São Saturnino	2

Azenhas do Mar

Praia das Maças

Praia Pequena

Praia Grande

Praia da Adraga

Ribeira da Sintra

Colares

Eugaria

Sintra

Almoçageme

Penedo

Monserrate

PARQUE NATURAL SINTRA-CASCAIS

Cabo da Roca

Azoia

Peninha

Convento dos Capuchos

Lagoa Azul

Penha Longa

Malveira da Serra

Autodrome

N

Praia do Guincho

Orbitur Guincho

0 kilometres 2

0 mile 1

Azenhas do Mar

lawn in Iberia, and it remains one of Europe's most richly stocked gardens, with over a thousand different species of subtropical tree and plant.

From the entrance, paths lead steeply down through lush undergrowth to a ruined chapel, half engulfed by a giant banyan tree. From here, lawns take you up to Cook's main legacy, a great **Victorian palace** inspired by Brighton Pavilion, with its mix of Moorish and Italian decoration – the dome is modelled on the Duomo in Florence. The interior has been restored after years of neglect, and you can now admire the amazingly intricate plasterwork which covers almost every wall and ceiling. The park also has a decent café (daily 10am–6pm).

Azenhas do Mar

MAP P.110
Bus #441 from Sintra (every 1–2hr; 40min).
Whitewashed cottages tumble down the steep cliff-face at the pretty village of **Azenhas do Mar**, one of the most lively villages of the Sintra coast. The beach is small, but there are artificial seawater pools for swimming in when the ocean is too rough.

Praia das Maçãs

MAP P.110
Bus #441 from Sintra (every 1–2hr; 30min); or Praia das Maças tram from Sintra (see box, p.112).
The largest and liveliest resort on this coast, **Praia das Maçãs** is also the easiest to reach from Sintra – take the tram (see box, page 112) for the most enjoyable journey. Along with a big swath of sand, there's an array of bars and restaurants to suit all budgets.

Praia Grande

MAP P.110
Bus #441 from Sintra (every 1–2hr; 25min).
Set in a wide, sandy cliff-backed bay, this is one of the best and safest **beaches** on the Sintra coast, though its breakers attract surfers aplenty. In August the World Bodyboarding Championships are held here, along with games such as volleyball and beach rugby. Plenty of inexpensive cafés and restaurants are spread out along the beachside road, and if the sea gets too rough, there are giant

sea pools on the approach to the beach (June–Sept; €10).

Praia da Adraga

MAP P.110

No public transport; by car, follow the signs from the village of Almocageme.
Praia da Adraga was flatteringly voted one of Europe's best beaches by a British newspaper; the unspoilt, cliff-backed, sandy bay with just one beach restaurant is certainly far quieter than the other resorts, but it takes the full brunt of the Atlantic, so you'll need to take great care when swimming.

Cabo da Roca

MAP P.110

Bus #403 from Sintra or Cascais train stations (roughly hourly; 45min).
Little more than a windswept **rocky cape** with a lighthouse, this is the most westerly point in mainland Europe, which guarantees a steady stream of visitors – get there early to avoid the coach parties. You can soak up the views from the café-restaurant and handicraft shop (daily 9.30am–7.30pm) and buy a certificate to prove you've been here at the little tourist office (daily 9am–7.30pm, closes 6.30pm from Oct–May; ☎ 219 280 081).

Convento dos Capuchos

MAP P.110

No public transport. A return taxi from Sintra with a 1hr stopover costs around €40 ☎ 219 237 381, ⓦ parquesdesintra.pt. Daily: March–Oct 9.30am–8pm; Nov–Feb 10am–6pm. €7.
If you have your own transport, don't miss a trip to the **Convento dos Capuchos**, an extraordinary hermitage with tiny, dwarf-like cells cut from the rock and lined with cork – hence its popular name of the Cork Convent. It was occupied for three hundred years until being finally abandoned in 1834 by its seven remaining monks, who must have found the gloomy warren of rooms and corridors too much to maintain. Some rooms – the penitents' cells – can only be entered by crawling through 70cm-high doors; here, and on every other ceiling, doorframe and lintel, are attached panels of cork, taken from the surrounding woods. Elsewhere, you'll come across a washroom, kitchen, refectory, tiny chapels, and even a bread oven set apart from the main complex.

Peninha

MAP P.110

With your own transport, it is worth exploring the dramatic wooded landscape between Capuchos and Cabo da Roca, much of it studded with giant moss-covered boulders. Some 3km from Capuchos lies **Peninha**, a spectacularly sited hermitage perched on a granite crag. The sixteenth-century Baroque interior is usually locked, but climb up anyway to get dazzling views of the Sintra coast towards Cascais. You can also take a waymarked 4.5km trail round the crag; otherwise it is a short return walk from the woodland car park.

Convento dos Capuchos

Restaurants

A Tasca do Manel

MAP P.110
Largo Dr. Virgílio Horta 5 ☎ 219 230 215.
Mon–Fri 7.30am–8pm, Sat 7.30am–7pm.
In total contrast to Sintra's wonderfully ornate Town Hall opposite, this is a simple but recommended little *tasca* with cured hams hanging over the bar. Squeeze into a table for good-value, no-nonsense fish, stews and grills from around €8.

Caldo Entornado

MAP P.110
Rua Guilherme Gomes Fernandes 19 ☎ 219 244 149, ⓦ caldo-entornado.pt. Daily 12.30–3pm & 7–10.30pm.
Attached to the *Moon Hill* hostel (see page 133), this cosy, good-value contemporary restaurant specializes in gourmet burgers of all descriptions, including salmon and cod varieties, as well as, of course, the usual beef patty (€7–10).

Cantinho de São Pedro

MAP P.110
Praça D. Fernando II 18, São Pedro de Sintra ☎ 219 230 267, ⓦ cantinhosaopedro. com. Daily noon–3pm & 7.30–10pm.
Large restaurant with bare stone walls overlooking an attractive courtyard just off São Pedro's main square. The traditional dishes (such as *bacalhau com natas*) are better than the international ones. Mains from €9. On cool evenings a log fire keeps things cosy.

Incomum

MAP P.110
Rua Dr. Alfredo Costa 22, Sintra ☎ 219 243 719, ⓦ incomumbyluissantos.pt. Mon–Fri & Sun noon–midnight, Sat 4.30pm–midnight.
Close to the station, this upmarket restaurant and wine bar is run by chef Luís Santos. His stints in some of Switzerland's top restaurants are reflected in a menu featuring the likes of scallops with mushroom risotto, black linguini with seafood and steak with sweet potatoes, though the ingredients are local and top quality. Mains from €15.

Páteo do Garrett

MAP P.110
Rua Maria Eugénia Reis F. Navarro 7 ☎ 219 243 380, ⓦ www.pateodogarrett. com. Mid-March to Oct daily 9.30am–10.30pm; Nov to mid-March Mon, Tues & Thurs–Sun 9.30am–6pm.
Although this café-restaurant has a dark, dim interior, it's also got a lovely sunny patio offering fine views over the village. Serves mixed meat kebabs, monkfish rice and the like from around €12–14, or just pop in for a drink.

Restaurante Regional de Sintra

MAP P.110
Trav do Município 2 ☎ 219 234 444. Mon, Tues & Thurs–Sun noon–4pm & 7–10.30pm.
In a lovely old building next to the Câmara Municipal, this traditional and slightly formal restaurant serves tasty dishes at reasonable prices – fresh fish from €12, grilled meats from €10–15 and a very good *crêpe de marisco* (seafood crêpe) for €10.

Tulhas

MAP P.110
Rua Gil Vicente 4–6 ☎ 219 232 378. Mon, Tues & Thurs–Sun noon–midnight.
Imaginative cooking in a fine building converted from old grain silos – the old grain well takes pride of place in the floor. The giant mixed grills at €40 for two will keep carnivores happy, while the weekend specials are usually good value, with meat and fish from around €12.

Cafés

Adega das Caves

MAP P.110
Rua da Pendoa 2–10 ☎ 219 230 848, ⓦ adegadascaves.com. Daily 10am–2am.
Bustling café-bar in the former palace coal merchants, attracting a

predominantly local and youthful clientele; the restaurant does meals from around €9.

Casa Piriquita

MAP P.110
Rua das Padarias 1 ☎ 219 230 626.
Mon, Tues & Thurs–Sun 9am–8pm.
Cosy tearoom and bakery, dating from 1862, which can get quite busy with locals queueing to buy the likes of *queijadas de Sintra* (sweet cheesecakes), *travesseiros* (doughy almond cakes) and other delicious pastries.

Fábrica das Verdadeiras Queijadas da Sapa

MAP P.110
Volta do Duche 12 ☎ 219 230 493.
Tues–Fri 9am–7pm, Sat & Sun 9am–8pm.
This old-fashioned café is famed for its traditional *queijadas*, made on the premises for over a century. It's a bit dingy inside, so buy a takeaway to eat on your walk to the centre.

Saudade

MAP P.110
Avda Dr. Miguel Bombarda 6, Sintra ☎ 212 428 804. Daily 8.30am–7pm.
This buzzy café used to be a factory selling *queijadas* and

Café Paris

has a warren of rooms and its own art gallery, with occasional live music. As well as cakes, scones and sandwiches, it serves some interesting *petiscos* such as Madeiran garlic bread and regional cheeses. A wide range of drinks and teas includes Gorreana tea from the Azores.

Bars

Bar Fonte da Pipa

MAP P.110
Rua Fonte da Pipa 11–13 ☎ 219 234 437.
Daily 9pm–3am.
Laidback bar with low lighting, comfy chairs and a fine sangria. It's up the hill from *Casa Piriquita*, next to the lovely ornate fountain (*fonte*) that the street is named after.

Café Paris

MAP P.110
Praçe da República 32 T219 232 375. Daily 9am–midnight.
This attractive blue-tiled café-bar is the highest-profile in the city, which means steep prices for not especially exciting food, although it is a great place to linger over a cocktail.

The Lisbon coast

Lisbon's most accessible beaches lie along the Cascais coast just beyond the point where the Tejo flows into the Atlantic. Famed for its casino, Estoril has the best sands, though neighbouring Cascais has more buzz. The River Tejo separates Lisbon from high-rise Caparica, to the south, on a superb stretch of wave-pounded beach, popular with surfers.

Estoril

MAP P.120

With its grandiose villas, luxury hotels and health spa, **Estoril** (pronounced é-stril) has pretensions towards being a Portuguese Riviera. The centre is focused on the leafy **Parque do Estoril** and its huge casino (daily 3pm–3am; free; semiformal attire required; ☎214 667 700, Ⓦcasino-estoril.pt). During World War II, this was where exiled royalty hung out and many spies made their names. Ian Fleming was based here to keep an eye on double agents, and used his experience at the casino as inspiration for the first James Bond novel, *Casino Royale*.

The resort's fine sandy beach, **Praia de Tamariz**, is backed by some ornate villas and a seafront promenade that stretches northwest to Cascais, a pleasant twenty-minute stroll. In summer, firework displays take place above the beach every Saturday at midnight.

Estoril is famed for its top **golf courses** which lie a short distance inland (info at Ⓦportugalgolf. pt); it also hosts the Estoril Open tennis tournament in May (Ⓦmillenniumestorilopen.com).

Cascais

MAP P.120

Cascais (pronounced cash-kaysh) is a highly attractive former fishing village, liveliest round Largo Luís

Tamariz beach in Estoril

Transport to Estoril and Cascais

Trains from Lisbon's Cais do Sodré (every 15–20min; 35min to Estoril, 40min to Cascais; €2.75 single) wend along the shore. There are also regular buses to and from Sintra, or it's a fine drive down the corniche.

de Camões, at one end of Rua Frederico Arouca, the main mosaic-paved pedestrian thoroughfare. **Praia da Conceição** is ideal to lounge on or try out watersports. The rock-fringed smaller beaches of **Praia da Rainha** and **Praia da Ribeira** are off the central stretch, while regular buses run 6km northwest to **Praia do Guincho**, a fabulous sweep of surf-beaten sands.

Cascais is at its most charming in the grid of streets north of the **Igreja da Assunção** – its *azulejos* predate the earthquake of 1755. Nearby, on Rua Júlio Pereira de Melo, the engaging **Museu do**

Mar (☎ 214 815 906; Tues–Fri 10am–5pm, Sat & Sun 10am–1pm & 2–5pm; free) relates the town's relationship with the sea, with model boats, treasure from local wrecks and stuffed fish.

Casa das Histórias

MAP P.119
Avda da República 300 ☎ 214 826 970,
ⓦ casadashistoriaspaularego.com.
Tues–Sun 10am–6pm. €5.

The distinctive ochre towers of the modernist **Casa das Histórias** mark a fantastic museum which, unusually, is dedicated to a living artist, Paula Rego. Designed by Eduardo Souto de Moura, the airy

Cascais

RESTAURANTS
B & B	6
Cafe Galeria House of Wonders	4
Jardim dos Frangos	2
O Pescador	3
O Solar do Bitoque	5
Taberna da Praça	7

CAFÉ
Santini	1

BAR
Chequers	2
Jonas Bar	1

Villa Shopping & Bus Station
Train Station
AVENIDA MARGINAL
★ Taxis
ALAMEDA DUQUESA PALMELA

Jardim Visconde da Luz
PRAÇA DR. FRANCISCO SÁ CARNEIRO
RUA I. DOYLE

AVENIDA VALBOM
RUA FREDERICO AROUCA
LARGO DA PRAIA DA RAINHA
Praia da Conceição

AV. COMB. DE GRANDE GUERRA
R. VISCONDE DA LUZ
R. AFONSO SANCHES
LARGO LUIS DE CAMÕES
R. POÇO NOVO
R. DOS NAVEGANTES
R. LATINO COELHO
RUA VITÓRIA
R. DA ALFARROBEIRA
R. MISERICÓRDIA
R. D. C. FLORES
R. DAS FLORES
LARGO 5 DE OUTUBRO
Praia da Ribeira
Town Hall ⓘ

Praia da Rainha

ATLANTIC OCEAN

R. VASCO DE GAMA
R. C. FERREIRA
R. A. RAPOSO
R. L. PALMEIRA
R. MANL DAL. I. BLADIM
AV. D. CARLOS I PASSEIO DOM LUIS I

Museu do Mar
Casa das Histórias
AV. DA REPÚBLICA
LARGO DA ASSUNÇÃO
Igreja da Assunção

N

Palácio da Cidadela
Pousada

Parque Municipal da Gandarinha

Marina de Cascais

R. J. PADILHO
R. PEL. DE OLIVEIRA
Museu Biblioteca Conde Castro Guimarães
ESTRADA DA BOCA DO INFERNO

AVENIDA REI HUMBERTO II DE ITÁLIA
Praia de Santa Marta
Santa Marta Lighthouse

0 metres	100
0 yards	100

ACCOMMODATION
Farol Design Hotel	5
Hotel Baía	2
Martinhal Cascais	4
Pergola House	1
Vila Bicuda	3

museum features over 120 of her disturbing but beautiful collages, pastels and engravings, as well as those by her late English husband Victor Willing. Many of her works explore themes of power: women and animals are portrayed as both powerful and sexually vulnerable; men often appear as fish or dressed in women's clothes.

Around Cascais Marina

MAP P.119

The leafy **Parque Municipal da Gandarinha**, complete with picnic tables and playground, makes a welcome escape from the beach crowds. In one corner stands the mansion of the nineteenth-century Count of Guimarães, preserved complete with its fittings as the **Museu Biblioteca Conde Castro Guimarães** (⊙ 214 825 401, ⓦ cm-cascais.pt; Tues–Sun 10am–5pm; closes 1–2pm on Sat and Sun; free). Its most valuable

exhibits are rare illuminated sixteenth-century manuscripts.

Palácio da Cidadela

MAP P.119

Avda Dom Carlos I ⊙ 213 614 660, ⓦ cascais.pt. Wed–Sun 11am–1pm & 2–6pm. €4

To the east, the walls of Cascais' largely seventeenth-century **Citadela** (fortress) guard the entrance to the **Marina de Cascais**, lined by restaurants, bars and boutiques.

Originally a sea fort and then a summer retreat for Portuguese royalty, the Citadela has been used by the Portuguese president to entertain his guests ever since the declaration of the Republic in 1910. Today, you can wander around the lower-floor exhibition space, though it's worth the entrance fee to visit the top two floors (ask for a non-guided visit unless you understand Portuguese). There's also a lovely ocean-facing tearoom.

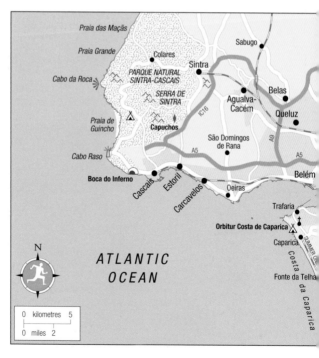

Caparica

MAP P.120
Via Rapida express 135 (roughly hourly; 30min) or slower local buses (every 15–30min; 50min), from Cacilhas or bus #161 from Lisbon's Areeiro (every 30–60min; 40–60min).

According to legend, **Caparica** was named after the discovery of a cloak (*capa*) full of golden coins. Today it is a slightly tacky, high-rise seaside resort, but don't let that put you off: it's family-friendly, has plenty of good seafood as well as several kilometres of soft, sandy beach.

From the beach, a **narrow-gauge mini-railway** (June–Sept daily every 30min from 9am–7.30pm; last return 7pm; €8 return, or €4.50 return for first nine stops) runs south along the beach for 8km to the resort of **Fonte da Telha**. Jump off at any stop en route; earlier stops tend to be family-oriented, while nudity is common in later ones.

Surfers on the Costa da Caparica coastline

Restaurants

B & B

MAP P.119

Rua do Poço Novo 15–17, Cascais ☎ 214 820 686. Mon–Sat noon–2.30pm & 6–9pm. A small, intimate diner in the old town, specializing in tender steaks (around €13). Also does a few fresh fish dishes, omelettes and salads and great desserts – save room for the chocolate cake.

Cafe Galeria House of Wonders

MAP P.119

Largo da Misericordia 53 ☎ 911 702 428. Daily 10am–10pm.

This Dutch-run veggie café-restaurant and gallery space has an appealing, alternative vibe. The street-level restaurant serves amazing vegetarian meze of various sizes from €8–15. Expect hummus, chickpea salad and whatever fresh veg is in season. There's a separate entrance for the gallery space and laidback café, complete with a roof terrace where you can relax for a drink on old packing cases.

Deck Bar

MAP P.119

Arcadas do Parque 21–22, Estoril ☎ 214 680 366. Tues–Sun 8am–2am. Facing Estoril's park, this great little café-restaurant and bar has appealing outdoor tables. It's a good spot for a drink or snack, and also

Cafe Galeria House of Wonders

serves a range of full meals (salads, tortilla, fresh fish) from around €10.

Jardim dos Frangos

MAP P.119

Avda Com. Grande Guerra 68 ☎ 214 861 717, Cascais. Daily 10am–11.30pm. Permanently buzzing with people and sizzling with the speciality, bargain grilled chicken from around €8, which is devoured at indoor and outdoor tables. Get there early to secure a table as it's very popular.

O Barbas - Catedral

Apoio de Praia 13, Caparica ☎ 212 900 163. Daily noon–midnight; Oct–April closes Wed. Caparica's best-known beach restaurant with affordable fish, *caldeirada* (fish stew) and *arroz de marisco* (seafood rice) to die for. They also run the more upmarket space next door, *O Barbas Tertúlia*, though the menu is much the same.

O Pescador

MAP P.119

Rua das Flores 10B, Cascais ☎ 214 832 054, ⓦ restaurantepescador.com. Wed 6–11pm, Thurs–Tues noon–11pm. The best of a row of lively restaurants near the centre, offering upmarket seafood – expect to pay over €40 for superb mains such as lobster baked in salt or tuna cooked in olive oil and garlic.

O Solar do Bitoque

MAP P.119

Rua Regimento 19 de Infantaria Loja 11, Cascais ☎ 918 580 343. Mon–Sat 10am–midnight.

This lively local with outdoor seating specializes in *bitoques* (thin steaks), as well as burgers, salads and fresh fish. Most dishes under €9.

Restaurante Praia do Tamariz

Praia do Tamariz, Estoril ☎ 214 681 010, ⓦ restaurantepraiadotamariz.com. Daily April–Oct 9am–10pm, Nov–March noon–6pm

High-profile restaurant right on the seafront promenade – which

Taberna da Praça

makes good-value fish, meat, pizza and pasta dishes (from around €12). Also a great spot for a sangria or *caipirinha*.

Taberna da Praça

MAP P.119
Cidadela de Cascais, Avda Dom Carlos I ① 214 814 300. Mon–Fri 12.30–3pm & 7.30–10.30pm, Sat & Sun noon–10.30pm.
Tucked into a couple of cosy arched rooms within Cascais's impressive fortress, *Taberna da Praça* serves a range of tasty *petiscos*, the Portuguese version of tapas. You can sample regional specialities like scrambled eggs with smoked chicken chorizo, or grilled octopus with baked potatoes (€4–10). There are also more substantial mains: great tuna steaks or duck rice (from €14).

Café

Santini

MAP P.119
Avda Valbom 28f ① 214 833 709. Mon–Thurs & Sun 11am–8pm, Fri & Sat 11am–midnight.
Opened by an Italian immigrant just after World War II, *Santini's*

delicious ice creams are legendary in these parts.

Bars and clubs

Chequers

MAP P.119
Largo Luís de Camões 7, Cascais ① 214 830 926. Daily 9.30–2am.
A laidback English-style pub that fills up early with a good-time crowd; it serves so-so meals too, with weekend DJs and live football matches screened on TV. However, most people tend to come here for relaxed drinks at the scattering of tables outside in the attractive square.

Jonas Bar

MAP P.119
Passeio Marítimo, Praia das Moitas Monte Estoril ① 214 676 946. Wed–Mon 10am–11pm (closes earlier in winter in bad weather).
Set right on the seafront just north of Estoril, this is an easygoing spot come day or night, serving a range of good food, tempting cocktails, fresh juices and snacks until the small hours.

ACCOMMODATION

Palacete Chafariz d'El Rei

Accommodation

Lisbon's hotels range from sumptuous five-stars to backstreet hideaways packed with local character. The grander ones tend to be found along Avenida da Liberdade, around Parque Eduardo VII or out of the centre, though in recent years around forty have opened in the central Baixa where there are now endless options. Besides its hotels, Lisbon still has a few old-style guesthouses (*alojamento local* or *particular*, some of which keep the now abandoned titles of *pensão* or *residencial*) and various good-value hostels. Over the past decade or so, a wave of boutique-style hotels and guesthouses have sprung up across the city, often in old townhouses that have been transformed into stylish accommodation – these are usually reasonably priced and make for an atmospheric and comfortable stay. The Alfama and Bairro Alto, too, are beginning to offer a greater choice, with crumbling buildings being done up into hotels or smart self-catering apartments – often with great city or river views thanks to the districts' hilltop positions. Given the surge in new accommodation, it's rarely hard to find a decent room, except in high season. Prices given are for a night in the cheapest double room in high season. Rates drop considerably out of season. Unless otherwise stated, all the places reviewed below have an en-suite bath or shower and include breakfast (anything from bread, jam and coffee to a generous spread of rolls, cereals, croissants, cold meat, cheese and fruit).

The Baixa and Rossio

ALBERGARIA INSULANA MAP P.26, POCKET MAP D12. Rua da Assunção 52 ⓌRossio ☎ 213 427 625, Ⓦinsulana. net. Go upstairs past a series of shops to reach one of the more quirky Baixa options. With its own bar overlooking a quiet pedestrianized street, the hotel's slightly faded rooms are complete with satellite TV and a/c. English-speaking staff. €97

ALMALUSA MAP P.26, POCKET MAP D13. Praça do Município 21, tram #28 to Praça do Município ☎ 212 697 440, Ⓦalmalusahotels.com. Beautifully positioned in the corner of a historic square, this eighteenth-century building now houses

Booking a room

The main tourist offices (see page 141) can provide accommodation lists, but won't reserve rooms for you. In the summer months, confirm a reservation at least a week in advance and get written confirmation; most owners understand English. Look out, too, for deals on hotel websites which are usually cheaper than walk-in rates.

Self-catering

There are several fine options for self-catering in Lisbon. As well as ⓦairbnb.co.uk, good first points of call are ⓦfadoflats. pt (mostly in Chiado and Alfama), ⓦcastleinnlisbon.com, which has apartments right by the castle, or ⓦtravellershouse.com, a hostel which also has four attractive apartments near Elevador da Lavra. Geared up to families is the upmarket Martinhal Chiado (ⓦmartinhal.com) in the Chiado district.

a chic boutique hotel. All the rooms are different, but each includes a smart TV and digital radio, and most have period touches such as flagstone floors and fireplaces. Front rooms overlook the town hall and tram routes. There's also a downstairs restaurant and small outdoor terrace. **€160**

HOTEL AVENIDA PALACE MAP P.26, POCKET MAP C11. Rua 1 de Dezembro 123 ⓦ Restauradores ☎ 213 218 100, ⓦ www. hotelavenidapalace.pt. Built at the end of the nineteenth century, and rumoured to have a secret door direct to neighbouring Rossio station, this is one of Lisbon's grandest hotels. Despite extensive modernization, the traditional feel has been maintained with chandeliers and period furniture throughout. There are 82 spacious rooms, each with high ceilings and colossal bathrooms. **€230**

HOTEL MÉTROPOLE MAP P.26, POCKET MAP D11. Rossio 30, ⓦ Restauradores ☎ 213 219 030, ⓦ metropole-lisbon.com. Welcoming three-star dating to the early twentieth century, with an airy lounge-bar offering superb views over Rossio and the castle. The simply furnished but spacious rooms are comfortable, though the square can be quite noisy at night. **€120**

PENSÃO PORTUENSE MAP P.26, POCKET MAP J5. Rua das Portas de Santo Antão 149–157 ⓦ Restauradores ☎ 213 464 197, ⓦ pensaoportuense.com. Singles, doubles and triples in a family-run guesthouse in a great position. Decently decorated, all rooms come with a/c and TV, and there's wi-fi access. **€102**

RESIDENCIAL FLORESCENTE MAP P.26, POCKET MAP J5. Rua das Portas de Santo Antão 99 ⓦ Restauradores ☎ 213 426 609, ⓦ residencialflorescente.com. The best

guesthouse on this pedestrianized street. There's a large selection of air-conditioned rooms across four floors (some en-suite with TV), so if you don't like the look of the room you're shown – and some are very cramped – ask about alternatives. Street-facing rooms can be noisy. There's also a lounge plus internet access for a small fee. **€102**

VIP EXECUTIVE ÉDEN MAP P.26, POCKET MAP C10. Praça dos Restauradores 24 ⓦ Restauradores ☎ 213 216 600, ⓦ viphotels.com. Compact studios and apartments sleeping up to four people are available within the impressively converted Éden cinema. Get a ninth-floor apartment with a balcony and you'll have the best views and be just below the superb breakfast bar and rooftop pool. All come with dishwashers, microwaves and satellite TV. Disabled access. **Studios from €100, breakfast extra**

The Sé, Castelo and Alfama

ALBERGARIA SENHORA DO MONTE MAP P.38, POCKET MAP L5. Calçada do Monte 39, Tram #28 ☎ 218 866 002, ⓦ albergaria-senhora-do-monte.lisbon-hotel.org. Comfortable, modern hotel in a sublime location with views of the castle and Graça convent from the south-facing rooms (avoid the north-facing ones), some of which have terraces. Breakfast is taken on the fourth-floor terrace. Free wi-fi and private parking are available. **€100**

MEMMO ALFAMA MAP P.38, POCKET MAP F12. Trav Merceeiras 27, Tram #28 ☎ 210 495 660, ⓦ www.memmoalfama. com. Hidden behind the facade of a former house, paint factory and bakery lies this sleek boutique hotel. Parts of the ground floor contain the old brick ovens, though

Author picks

BUDGET *Home Hostel* see page 133
DESIGNER *Memmo Alfama* see page 127
RETRO CHIC *Heritage Avenida* see page 130
FAMILY *Lisboa Plaza* see page 131
HISTORIC *Palacete Chafariz d'el Rei* see page 128

the real appeal is the bar with terraces at the back, complete with small plunge pool, offering sumptuous views over the Alfama and the Tagus. Rooms are compact, but have all mod cons and most boast fine views. **€235**

PALACETE CHAFARIZ D'EL REI MAP P.38, POCKET MAP G12. Trav Chafariz d'El Rei 6, Tram #25 ☎ 218 886 150, ⓦ chafarizdelrei. com. Luxury guesthouse built in 1909 by a wealthy Brazilian merchant and lovingly restored a century later. From the reception – flooded with light from stained-glass windows – to the mirror room and library, the house is a stunning mix of Brazilian Art Nouveau and neo-Arabic flamboyance. Huge rooms, most with river views, have chandeliers and modern bathrooms while stonking breakfasts keep you going till dinner time. **€342**

SOLAR DO CASTELO MAP P.38, POCKET MAP F11. Rua das Cozinhas 2, Bus #37 ☎ 218 806 050, ⓦ solardocastelo.com. A tastefully renovated eighteenth-century mansion abutting the castle walls on the site of the former palace kitchens, parts of which remain. Its 14 rooms cluster around a tranquil inner courtyard, where you can enjoy a vast buffet breakfast. Rooms aren't enormous, but most boast balconies overlooking the castle grounds, and service is second to none. **€165**

SOLAR DOS MOUROS MAP P.38, POCKET MAP F12. Rua do Milagre de Santo António 6, Tram #28 ☎ 218 854 940, ⓦ solardosmouroslisboa.com. A tall Alfama townhouse done out in a contemporary style with its own bar. Each of the twelve rooms offers fantastic vistas of the river or castle and comes with CD player and a/c. There's plenty of modern art to enjoy if you tire of the view. **€190**

Chiado and Cais do Sodré

HOTEL BAIRRO ALTO MAP P.52, POCKET MAP C12. Praça Luís de Camões 2 Ⓜ Baixa-Chiado ☎ 213 408 223, ⓦ bairroaltohotel.com. In the middle of trendy Chiado, this grand eighteenth-century building has been modernized into a fashionable boutique hotel. Rooms and communal areas still have a period feel, but a fantastic contemporary extension by architect Eduardo Souto de Moura brings the building into the twenty-first century. The rooms have all the luxuries you'd expect, with great views from the top-floor ones – and from the rooftop café-bar. **€230**

HOTEL BORGES MAP P.52, POCKET MAP C12. Rua Garrett 108 Ⓜ Baixa-Chiado ☎ 210 456 400, ⓦ hotelborges.com. In a prime spot on Chiado's main street, this traditional and elegantly furnished three-star is very popular, though front rooms can be noisy. Double or triple rooms are plain and small but good value. **€110**

HOTEL DO CHIADO MAP P.52, POCKET MAP D12. Rua Nova do Almada 114 Ⓜ Baixa-Chiado ☎ 213 256 100, ⓦ hoteldochiado.pt. Designed by architect Álvaro Siza Vieira, this stylish hotel has lovely communal areas – orange segment-shaped windows give glimpses of Chiado in one direction and the whole city in the other. The cheapest rooms lack much of an outlook, but the best ones have terraces with stunning views towards the castle – a view you get from the bar terrace too. All rooms have wi-fi. Limited parking available. **€190**

LX BOUTIQUE MAP P.52, POCKET MAP C13. Rua do Alecrim 12 Ⓜ Cais do Sodré ☎ 213 474 394, ⓦ lxboutiquehotel.pt. A tasteful makeover to an old townhouse has transformed *LX Boutique* into a popular small hotel with its own chic restaurant.

The "boutique" refers to its themed floors, named after Portuguese poets and fado singers. Rooms are all stylish and individual, with shutters and tasteful lighting – try and get one with river views rather than over the late-night Rua Nova do Carvalho. **€165**

Bairro Alto and São Bento

CASA DE SÃO MAMEDE MAP P.60, POCKET MAP H5. Rua da Escola Politécnica 159, Bus #1 ☎ 213 963 166, Ⓦ casadesaomamede.pt. On a busy street north of Príncipe Real, this is a superb eighteenth-century former magistrate's house with period fittings, bright breakfast room and a grand stained-glass window. Rooms are rather ordinary, but all are equipped with a TV and a/c. **€100**

HOTEL ANJO AZUL MAP P.60, POCKET MAP B11. Rua Luz Soriano 75, Bus #1 ☎ 213 478 069, Ⓦ anjoazul.com. The "Blue Angel" is best known for being LGBTQ-friendly, but is not exclusively so. Set in a lovely blue-tiled townhouse right in the heart of the area's nightlife, 20 simple but attractive rooms are set over four floors (€50), most with en-suite facilities (€65). No breakfast; however, there is a living room. **€60**

HOTEL BELVER PRINCÍPE REAL MAP P.60, POCKET MAP H5. Rua da Alegria 53, Bus #1 ☎ 213 407 350, Ⓦ hotelprincipereal.belverhotels.net. This small four-star sits on a quiet street just below the Bairro Alto. Eighteen rooms come with modern decor, some with balconies and superb city views. Best of all is the top-floor suite with stunning vistas. **€140**

THE INDEPENDENTE HOSTEL & SUITES MAP P.60, POCKET MAP B10. Rua de São Pedro de Alcântara 81 ☎ 213 461 381, Ⓦ theindependente.pt. This part-hostel, part-boutique hotel is set in a fantastic old building with far-reaching views over Lisbon. Lower floors house dorms (sleeping 6–12), each with towering ceilings. Upstairs are quirky double rooms in the roof spaces, the best with balconies offering river views. There's a downstairs bar and patio, and the place offers everything from bar crawls to guided walks and cycle hire. The

Suites element is in the building next door, offering larger rooms, a library and a hip bar on the roof terrace. **Dorms from €21, doubles and suites from €138**

PENSÃO GLOBO MAP P.60, POCKET MAP B10. Rua do Teixeira 37, Bus #1 ☎ 213 462 279, Ⓦ pensaoglobo.com. Attractive house on a relatively quiet street, bang in the middle of the Bairro Alto. Fifteen varied rooms: all are simple (including a box room for just €25), though avoid those without windows. There's a bar downstairs. No breakfast. **€40**

PENSÃO LONDRES MAP P.60, POCKET MAP B10. Rua Dom Pedro V 53, Bus #1 ☎ 213 462 203, Ⓦ pensaolondres.com.pt. Wonderful old building with high ceilings and pleasant enough rooms sleeping up to four. Some have tiny bathrooms, but the best (ask for rooms 402, 409 or 411) have great views over the city. **€60**

Estrela, Lapa and Santos

AS JANELAS VERDES MAP P.73, POCKET MAP G8. Rua das Janelas Verdes 47, Bus #727 or tram #25 ☎ 213 968 143, Ⓦ asjanelasverdes.com. This discreet eighteenth-century townhouse, where Eça de Queirós was inspired to write *Os Maias*, is just metres from the Museu de Arte Antiga. The spacious rooms come with marble bathrooms and period furnishings, most with views of the Tejo. Breakfast is served in the delightful walled garden in summer, while the top-floor library and terrace command spectacular river views. **€143**

OLISSIPPO LAPA PALACE MAP P.73, POCKET MAP F7. Rua do Pau da Bandeira 4 ☎ 213 949 494, Ⓦ lapapalace.com. A stunning nineteenth-century mansion set in its own lush gardens, with dramatic vistas over the Tejo. Rooms are luxurious, and those in the Palace Wing are each decorated in a different style, from Classical to Art Deco. There's also a health club, disabled access and a list of facilities as long as your arm, from babysitting to banqueting. **€285**

YORK HOUSE MAP P.73, POCKET MAP G7. Rua das Janelas Verdes 32, Bus #727 or tram #25 ☎ 213 962 435, Ⓦ yorkhouselisboa.com. Located in a sixteenth-century Carmelite convent (and hidden from the main street by high walls), rooms here are chic and minimalist. The best are grouped around a beautiful interior courtyard, where drinks and meals are served in summer, and there's a highly rated restaurant. Advance bookings recommended. €137

Alcântara and Belém

JERÓNIMOS 8 MAP P.78, POCKET MAP C4. Rua das Jerónimos 8, Tram #15 ☎ 213 600 900, Ⓦ jeronimos8.com. In a great position for Belém's attractions, this hotel is housed in an attractive stone building with boutiquey touches – crisp white decor, marble bathrooms and a modern bar area, plus a substantial buffet breakfast. €210

PESTANA PALACE MAP P.78, POCKET MAP C8. Rua Jau 54, Tram #18 ☎ 213 615 600, Ⓦ pestanapalacelisbon.com. Set in an early twentieth-century palace full of priceless works of art, most beds at this five-star hotel are in tasteful modern wings that stretch either side of lush gardens. Most rooms have large terraces and lie a short walk from a cocktail bar, a sunken outdoor pool with a fountain to swim out to, and an indoor pool and health club. The price, which can be greatly reduced for summer offers, includes a vast breakfast in the former ballroom. €266

Avenida, Parque Eduardo VII and the Gulbenkian

CASA AMORA MAP P.92, POCKET MAP G5. Rua João Penha 13 Ⓜ Rato ☎ 919 300 317, Ⓦ casaamora.com. This lovingly renovated townhouse lies close to the picturesque Praça das Amoreiras. There are five tastefully furnished rooms in the main house and six larger studios in a separate building which are suitable for families. There's also an attractive outdoor patio. €135

DOUBLE TREE FONTANA PARK MAP P.92, POCKET MAP J3. Rua Eng. Viera da Silva 2 Ⓜ Saldanha ☎ 210 410 600, Ⓦ doubletree3.hilton.com. This buzzy designer hotel rises sleekly behind the facade of an old steelworks. Chic rooms – the best with terraces – come with Philippe Starck chromatic baths. The communal areas include a restaurant, bar and a courtyard garden with slate walls of running water. Cocktail nights with guest DJs complete the picture. €107

EUROSTAR DAS LETRAS MAP P.92, POCKET MAP H5. Rua Castilho 6–12 Ⓜ Avenida ☎ 213 573 094, Ⓦ eurostarshotels.com. Modern hotel with its own small gym and bar in a good position between the centre and the Bairro Alto. Rooms, named after writers, come with comfy beds, a choice of pillows and a complicated array of power showers. The best have balconies with downtown views. €150

HERITAGE AVENIDA LIBERDADE MAP P.92, POCKET MAP J5. Avda da Liberdade 28 Ⓜ Restauradores ☎ 213 404 040, Ⓦ heritageavliberdade.com. In a fine mansion – whose ground floor once sold herbal remedies (the counter still remains) – this hotel superbly blends tradition and contemporary style. Though the dining area/bar is small (and the gym/plunge pool even smaller), the rooms more than compensate with retro fittings and great cityscapes from top-floor rooms. €195

HOTEL AVENIDA PARK MAP P.92, POCKET MAP H4. Avda Sidónio Pais 6 Ⓜ Parque ☎ 213 532 181, Ⓦ avenidapark. com. Good-sized rooms – beg for one with a view over the park for no extra charge – in a friendly, if dated, hotel on a quiet street. €80

HOTEL BRITANIA MAP P.92, POCKET MAP J5. Rua Rodrigues Sampaio 17 Ⓜ Avenida ☎ 213 155 016, Ⓦ hotel-britania.com. Designed in the 1940s by influential architect Cassiano Branco, this Art Deco gem features huge airy rooms, each with traditional cork flooring and marble-clad bathrooms. The hotel interior, with library and bar, has been declared of national architectural importance. €160

HOTEL DOM CARLOS PARQUE MAP P.92, POCKET MAP H4. Avda Duque de Loulé 121 Ⓜ Marquês de Pombal ☎ 213 512 590, Ⓦ hoteldomcarlospark.com. Decent three-star just off Praça Marquês de Pombal, with fair-sized rooms over eight floors, each with cable TV. Some overlook the neighbouring police and fire stations, which can add to the noise. There's a downstairs bar and garage parking. **€110**

INSPIRA SANTA MARTA MAP P.92, POCKET MAP J4. Rua de Santa Marta 48 ☎ 210 440 900, ⓦ inspirahotels.com. The facade of a traditional townhouse hides a modern boutique hotel which boasts impressive green credentials, including low-energy lighting and recycled or local products. Feng shui-designed rooms are compact but comfy with glass-wall showers, coffee-making facilities and free minibars. There's also a spa, games room, stylish restaurant and bar. **€140**

LISBOA PLAZA MAP P.92, POCKET MAP J5. Trav Salitre 7 ⓜ Avenida ☎ 213 218 218, ⓦ lisbonplazahotel.com. A tasteful, understated former Portuguese family home with marble bathrooms, a bar and fashionable rooftop terrace, a short walk from the main Avenida. Friendly staff and good for families. Limited disabled access. **€120**

NH LIBERDADE MAP P.92, POCKET MAP J5. Avda da Liberdade 180b ⓜ Avenida ☎ 213 514 060, ⓦ nh-hotels.com. Discreetly tucked into the back of the Tivoli forum shopping centre off the main Avenida, this Spanish chain hotel offers ten floors of modern flair. The best rooms have balconies facing the traditional Lisbon houses at the back. Unusually for central Lisbon, there's a rooftop pool. There's also a bar and restaurant. **€200**

SANA REX MAP P.92, POCKET MAP G4. Rua Castilho 169 ⓜ Marquês de Pombal/ Parque ☎ 213 882 161, ⓦ rex.sanahotels. com. One of the less outrageously priced hotels in this neck of the woods, with small but well-equipped rooms and a bar. The best rooms are at the front, sporting balconies overlooking Parque Eduardo VII. **€100**

SHERATON LISBOA MAP P.92, POCKET MAP J3. Rua Latino Coelho 1 ⓜ Picoas ☎ 213 120 000, ⓦ sheratonlisboa.com. This 1970s high-rise is something of an icon in this part of Lisbon and a mecca for those seeking five-star spa facilities. The dated exterior hides modern attractions, including a heated outdoor pool, swanky rooms and a top-floor bar and restaurant. **€180**

Sintra

CASA DO VALLE MAP P.110. Rua da Paderna 2 ☎ 219 244 699, ⓦ casadovalle. com. Though steeply downhill from the historic centre, this charming guesthouse still commands unbeatable views across the wooded slopes of Sintra. There are various rooms, from top-floor doubles with the best views, to ground-floor rooms with their own terraces. All rooms access a beautiful garden with its own pool. Good for families. **€90**; breakfast €6 extra

CHALET RELOGIO MAP P.110. Estrada da Pena 22, Sintra-Vila ☎ 219 243 539, ⓦ chalet-relogio-pt.book.direct. Architect Luigi Manini, who worked on the Quinta da Regaleira (see page 111), designed this mansion with a distinctive clock tower. Rooms are simply furnished but enormous, with big windows and high ceilings, and there's a garden too, though it's a long walk to town and you'll need a car. **€99**

CHALET SAUDADE MAP P.110. Rua Dr. Alfredo Costa 21 ☎ 210 150 055. This tall eighteenth-century chalet has been superbly renovated by a Portuguese couple who have retained many of the quirky but charming original fittings. The interior is all parquet flooring, swirling stairways, stained glass and beautiful *azulejos*. Stairs take you down three floors to rooms of varying sizes: it's best to pay €10 extra to bag the one opening onto the garden. Breakfast (€10 extra) is offered at *Saudade Café* (see page 117). **€70**

HOTEL ARRIBAS MAP P.110. Avda A Coelho 28, Praia Grande ☎ 219 289 050, ⓦ hotelarribas.pt. This three-star is plonked ungraciously above the beach. Large rooms come with minibars and satellite TV – those with a sea view are hard to fault – while family rooms sleep up to four. There are also seawater swimming pools, a restaurant and café terrace. Disabled access. **€135**

HOTEL NOVA SINTRA MAP P.110. Largo Afonso de Albuquerque 25, Estefânia

📞 219 230 220, 🌐 novasintra.com. A friendly hotel in a big mansion, whose elevated terrace-café overlooks a busy street. The modern rooms all have cable TV and shiny marble floors, and there's a decent restaurant. **€100**

HOTEL SINTRA JARDIM MAP P.110. Trav dos Avelares 12, São Pedro 📞 219 230 738, 🌐 hotelsintrajardim.pt. The best mid-range option in the area, this rambling old hotel has soaring ceilings, wooden floors and oodles of character. There's a substantial garden with a swimming pool, and the giant rooms can easily accommodate extra beds – so it's great for families. Book ahead in summer; in winter there's a log fire in the communal lounge. **€85, €10 extra for garden views**

SÃO SATURNINO MAP P.110. Azóia 📞 219 238 192, 🌐 saosat.com. Reached down a steep track – look for the sign left just past the turning to Cabo da Roca, before Azóia – this former convent dates back to the twelfth century and sits in a valley where time seems to stand still. The six rooms, three suites and self-catering apartment are traditionally furnished, while the rambling communal areas are all weathered beams, bare bricks and low ceilings. There's a small outdoor pool, barbecue area, geese, cats, and terraces with stunning views – truly magical. **€140**

Lisbon coast

FAROL DESIGN HOTEL MAP P.119. Avda Rei Humberto II de Italia 7, Cascais 📞 214 823 490, 🌐 farol.com.pt. Right on the seafront, this is one of the area's most fashionable hideaways, neatly combining traditional and contemporary architecture. A new designer wing has been welded onto a sixteenth-century villa, and the decor combines wood and marble with modern steel and glass. The best rooms have sea views and terraces. There's also a restaurant, fairy-lit outside bar and seapool facing a fine rocky foreshore. **€330/415 with sea views**

HOTEL BAÍA MAP P.119. Avda Marginal, Cascais 📞 214 831 033, 🌐 hotelbaia.com. Large seafront hotel boasting 113 rooms with a/c and satellite TV; front ones have balconies overlooking the beach. There's a great rooftop terrace complete with a covered pool, and a good restaurant. Parking charged extra. **€130/165 with sea view**

MARTINHAL CASCAIS MAP P.119. Quinta da Marinha, Rua do Clube 2750–002 Cascais 📞 211 149 900, 🌐 martinhal.com/cascais. Very smart contemporary hotel rooms and villas in a lovely wooded family-friendly complex on the outskirts of Cascais. With indoor and outdoor pools, a great spa, an excellent restaurant, tennis courts, kids' club and bike rental, it caters brilliantly for both parents and children. **€273**

PERGOLA HOUSE MAP P.119. Avda Valbom 13, Cascais 📞 214 840 040, 🌐 pergolahouse.pt. Sumptuous century-old mansion in the centre of town, with its own garden, stucco ceilings and ornate tiled dining room. Each room has its own distinct character, some with its own balcony. **€165**

REAL CAPARICA HOTEL Rua Mestre Manuel 18, Caparica 📞 212 918 870, 🌐 realcaparicahotel.com. Friendly and reasonable central hotel, a few minutes' walk from the beach, just off Rua dos Pescadores. Small but pleasant rooms come with TVs and baths, and some have balconies and sea views. **€80, €95 with sea view**

VILA BICUDA MAP P.119. Rua dos Faisões, Cascais 📞 214 860 200, 🌐 vilabicuda.com. A very well-run, upmarket villa complex set in its own grounds, with two large swimming pools. Excellent for families, the modern villas are well equipped and the complex has its own great café, shop and (pricey) Italian restaurant. But you'll need a car – it's around 3km from central Cascais towards Guincho. **Studios from €167**

Hostels

THE DORM MAP P.78, POCKET MAP D8. Rua Rodrigues de Faria 103 📞 211 346 746, 🌐 thedorm.pt. Funky hostel with industrial decor housed in an old textile printing plant in the hipster LX Factory complex. Spotless and good value, its cubbyhole-style dorms have chipboard dividers and small but comfy beds wedged into pigeonholes with lockers. There are also two double rooms, plus plush communal bathrooms and a stylish kitchen and living room to chill out in. **Dorm beds from €22, doubles from €65**

HOME HOSTEL MAP P.26, POCKET MAP E12. Rua de São Nicolau 13-2 ⊕ 218 885 312, Ⓦ homelisbonhostel.com. Located in the heart of the Baixa, this highly rated hostel comes with fantastic home-cooking, a buzzy communal lounge and the opportunity to sign up to walking tours and pub nights. **Four, six or eight-bed dorms from €32**

LISBON LOUNGE HOSTEL MAP P.26, POCKET MAP D12. Rua de São Nicolau 41 Ⓜ Rossio ⊕ 213 462 061, Ⓦ lisbonloungehostel.com. A popular independent hostel in a great old Baixa townhouse full of stripped floorboards, comfy sofas and books. Free wi-fi, and breakfast and dinner on request. **Dorm beds from €30, twins from €34**

MOON HILL HOSTEL MAP P.110. Rua Guilherme Gomes Fernandes 17, Sintra ⊕ 219 243 755, Ⓦ moonhillhostel.com. This fantastic hostel has friendly staff, stylish decor and a range of contemporary rooms, from en-suite doubles to dorms with bunk beds. There's a communal kitchen and lounge with a wood burner for the winter and a terrace and patio to unwind in the summer. **Dorms from €22, doubles from €70**

OASIS HOSTEL MAP P.60, POCKET MAP A12. Rua Santa Catarina 24 Ⓜ Baixa-Chiado/Tram #28 ⊕ 213 478 044, Ⓦ oasislisboa.com. In a lovely townhouse with its own patio garden, this independent hostel is a stone's throw from the fashionable Miradouro de Santa

Catarina. **Dorm beds from €25, doubles from €84**

POUSADA DE JUVENTUDE DE LISBOA MAP P.92, POCKET MAP H3. Rua Andrade Corvo 46 Ⓜ Picoas ⊕ 213 532 696, Ⓦ pousadasjuventude.pt. The main city hostel, housed in a rambling old building, with a small bar (open 6pm to midnight), canteen, TV room and disabled access. There are 30 dorms sleeping four to six, as well as en-suite rooms. Price includes breakfast. **Dorm beds from €18, doubles from €51**

POUSADA DE JUVENTUDE DE OEIRAS Estrada Marginal, Oeiras ⊕ 214 430 638, Ⓦ pousadasjuventude.pt. This hostel is set in an eighteenth-century sea-fort overlooking the sea pools in Oeiras, a suburb on the train line to Cascais. Reception is open 8am to midnight. Parking available. **Dorm beds from €13, twin rooms from €38**

POUSADA DE JUVENTUDE LISBOA PARQUE DAS NAÇÕES MAP P.104, POCKET MAP A16. Rua de Moscavide 47–101, Parque das Nações Ⓜ Oriente ⊕ 218 920 890, Ⓦ pousadasjuventude.pt. Located about five minutes' walk northeast of the Torre Vasco da Gama, towards the bridge, this smart and modern youth hostel has a pool table and disabled access. **Dorm beds from €17.50, doubles from €42**

TRAVELLERS HOUSE MAP P.26, POCKET MAP D12. Rua Augusta 89-1 Ⓜ Baixa-Chiado ⊕ 210 115 922, Ⓦ travellershouse. com. Right on Lisbon's main pedestrianized street, this award-winning independent hostel has a wonderful lounge, bean bags, a DVD room and appealing en-suite doubles. **Dorm beds from €26, doubles and studios from €90**

Lisbon hostels

Lisbon and its surroundings have some of Europe's best independent hostels. A youth hostel card is required for the official Portuguese hostels (*pousadas de juventude*), but you can buy one on your first night's stay. Unless stated, prices do not include breakfast.

ESSENTIALS

Pastéis de nata

Arrival

Lisbon airport is right on the edge of the city and is well served by buses and taxis. The city's train stations are all centrally located and connected to the metro; the main bus station is also close to metro and train stops.

By plane

Humberto Delgado Airport, or Lisbon Airport, (☎ 218 413 500, ⓦ ana.pt) is a twenty-minute drive north of the city centre and has a tourist office (☎ 218 450 660; daily 7am–midnight), a 24hr exchange bureau and left-luggage facilities.

   The easiest way in to the centre is by taxi; a journey to Rossio should cost around €15. The airport is also on the red Oriente line of the **metro** (see opposite), although you'll need to change at Alameda for the centre. Alternatively, catch Line 1 **Aerobus** (☎ 966 298 558, ⓦ aerobus.pt; daily every 20–30min, from 7.30am–11pm, €4, ticket valid for travel on all city buses for that day) from outside the terminal, which runs to Praça da Figueira, Praça do Comércio, Cais do Sodré train station, Rossio and Praça dos Restauradores. **Local bus** #744 also runs to Praça Marquês de Pombal (every 10–15min; €1.90), but is less convenient if you have a lot of luggage.

By train

Long-distance **trains** are run by CP (Comboios de Portugal; ☎ 707 210 220 or ☎ 351 707 210 220 from abroad, ⓦ cp.pt). You'll arrive at Santa Apolónia station, from where you can access the Gaivota metro line or take a bus west to Praça do Comércio. Some trains stop at Entrecampos (on the Amarela line) or at Oriente station (on the Oriente line) at Parque das Nações. These stations are more convenient for the airport or northern Lisbon.

By bus

The national **bus** carrier is Rede Expressos (☎ 707 223 344, ⓦ www.rede-expressos.pt). Most services terminate at Sete Rios, next to the Jardim Zoológico metro stop (for the centre) and Sete Rios train line (for Sintra and the northern suburbs). Some bus services also stop at the Oriente station at Parque das Nações on the Oriente metro line.

By car

Apart from weekends, when the city is quiet, **driving** round Lisbon is best avoided, though it is useful to hire a car to see the outlying sights. Parking is difficult in central Lisbon. Pay-and-display spots get snapped up quickly and the unemployed get by on tips for guiding drivers into empty spots. It may be easier heading for an official car park, for which you pay around €2.50 an hour or €15 a day. Do not leave valuables inside your car.

Getting around

Central Lisbon is compact enough to explore on **foot**, but don't be fooled by the apparent closeness of sights as they appear on maps. There are some very steep hills to negotiate, although the city's quirky *elevadores* (funicular railways) will save you the steepest climbs. Tram, bus and *elevador* stops are indicated by a sign marked "paragem", which carries route details.

   Metro stations (ⓜ) are located close to most of the main sights. Suburban trains run from Rossio and Sete Rios stations to Sintra and from Cais do Sodré station to Belém, Estoril and Cascais, while ferries (☎ 213 478 030, ⓦ www.

transtejo.pt) link Lisbon's Cais do Sodré to Cacilhas, for the resort of Caparica.

The metro

Lisbon's efficient **metro** (Metropolitano; daily 6.30–1am; ☎ 213 500 115, Ⓦ www.metrolisboa. pt) is the quickest way of reaching the city's main sights, with trains every few minutes. Tickets cost €1.45 per journey, or €1.31 with a Viva Viagem card (see below) – sold at all stations (see the inside cover and pull-out map for the network diagram).

Buses and trams

City trams and buses (daily 6.30am–midnight) are operated by Carris (☎ 213 500 115, Ⓦ carris.pt). **Buses** (*autocarros*) run just about everywhere in the Lisbon area – the most useful ones are outlined in the box below.

Trams (*eléctricos*) run on five routes, which are marked on the chapter maps. Ascending some of the steepest urban gradients in the world, most are worth taking for the ride alone, especially the cross-city tram #28 (see page 42). Another picturesque route is #12, which circles the castle area via Largo Martim Moniz. Other useful routes are "supertram" #15 from Praça da Figueira to Belém (signed Algés), and #18, which runs from Cais do Sodré via Praça do Comércio to the Palácio da Ajuda. The remaining route, #25, runs from near the Praça da Figueira to Campo Ourique via Santos, Lapa and Estrela.

Elevadores

There are also several **elevadores**. These consist of two funicular railways offering quick access to the heights of the Bairro Alto (see pages and 59) and to the eastern side of Avenida da Liberdade (see page 90); and one giant lift, the Elevador da Santa Justa (see page 29) which goes up to the foot of the Bairro Alto near Chiado. There are also free street lifts offering access to the lower edges of the Castelo de São Jorge (see map page 38).

Tickets and passes

On board **tickets** cost €1.85 (buses), €2.85 (trams) and €3.70 for *elevadores* (valid for two trips) and €5.15 for the Elevador da Santa Justa. You need to get a separate card for train lines to Sintra or Cascais. Note that the modern tram #15 has an automatic ticket machine on board and does not issue change.

It's possible just to buy a ticket each time you ride, but **passes**, available from any main metro station, can save you money. First, buy a rechargeable Viva Viagem card (€0.50), which you can load up with up to €3–40, after which €1.31 is deducted for each bus or metro journey.

You can also buy a one-day Bilhete 1dia pass (€6.30, or €10.40 including trains to Sintra and Cascais), which allows unlimited travel on buses, trams, the metro and *elevadores* for 24 hours after it is first used.

Useful bus routes

#201 Night bus from Cais do Sodré to the docks via Santos; until 5am.
#728 Belém to Parque das Nações via Santa Apolónia station.
#737 Praça da Figueira to Castelo de São Jorge via the Sé and Alfama.
#744 Outside the airport to Marquês de Pombal via Saldanha and Picoas (for the youth hostel).
#727 Marquês de Pombal to Belém via Santos and Alcântara.
#773 Rato to Alcântara via Príncipe Real, Estrela and Lapa.

If you're planning some intensive sightseeing, the Cartão Lisboa (ⓦwww.lisboacard.org; €19 for one day, €32 for two days, €40 for three, valid for one year) is a good buy. The card entitles you to unlimited rides on buses, trams, *elevadores* and the metro as well as entry to or discounts on around 25 museums. It's available online and from all the main tourist offices.

Taxis

Lisbon's cream **taxis** have a minimum charge of €3.25; an average ride across town is €10–15. Fares are twenty percent higher from 9pm to 6am, at weekends and on public holidays. Bags in the boot incur a €1.60 fee. Meters should be switched on, and tips are not expected. Outside the rush hour taxis can be flagged down quite easily, or head for one of the ranks such as those outside the main train stations. At night, it's best to phone a taxi (attracts an extra charge of €0.80): try Teletaxis (☎ 218 111 100, ⓦteletaxis.pt).

Car rental

For more information on driving in Lisbon see page 136. Rental agents include: Auto Jardim, airport ☎ 218 463 187, ⓦautojardimrentacar.pt; Avis/Budget, ☎ 213 514 560, airport ☎ 218 435 550, ⓦavis.com/budget.com; Europcar, ☎ 210 532 783, airport ☎ 218 401 176, ⓦeuropcar.com; Hertz, airport ☎ 219 426 300, ⓦhertz.com.

Sightseeing tours

Open-top bus tour The 1hr 40min "Circuito Tejo" departs from Praça da Figueira (June–Sept every 15min 9am–8pm; Oct–May every 20min 9am–5.30pm; €16) taking passengers around Lisbon's principal sights; a day-ticket allows you to get on and off whenever you want. (Information ☎ 213 478 030, ⓦyellowbustours.com.)

Tourist tram tours The "Elétrico das Colinas" (Hills Tour) takes passengers on a ninety-minute ride in an early twentieth-century tram (June–Sept every 25min 9.30am–7pm; Oct–May every 30min 9.30am–5.30pm; €19), departing from Praça do Comércio and touring around Alfama, Chiado and the Bairro Alto. (Information ☎ 213 478 030, ⓦyellowbustours.com.)

River cruises Various boat tours take in the sights of Lisbon from the river: the hop-on, hop-off Yellow Boat Tour leaves from Praça do Comércio and runs a ninety-minute trip beneath the Ponte 25 de Abril and out to Belém (May–Oct daily on the hour 10am–6pm; €18). (Information ☎ 213 478 030, ⓦyellowbustours.com.)

Jeep tours Head round the city in a Portuguese-built, open-top military jeep, able to negotiate some of the city's tortuous hills and alleys that buses can't reach. Various tours from €45 (☎ 913 776 598, ⓦwehatetourismtours.com.)

Walks Recommended themed two- to three-hour guided walks are offered by Lisbon Walker (☎ 218 861 840, ⓦwww.lisbonwalker.com; €15), departing daily from Praça do Comércio at 10am or 2.30pm, giving expert insight into the quirkier aspects of the city's sites, including secret histories and spies.

Tuk-tuk tours Various companies offer tours in three-wheeled tuk-tuks that can negotiate Lisbon's steepest and narrow streets around the Alfama. Prices start at around €45 an hour and depart from outside the Sé cathedral and also Sintra train station.

Directory A–Z

Addresses

Addresses are written in the form "Rua do Crucifixo 50–4°", meaning the fourth storey of no. 50, Rua do Crucifixo. The addition of e, d or r/c at the end means the entrance is on the left (*esquerda*), right (*direita*) or on the ground floor (*rés-do-chão*).

Bike hire

Most of Lisbon is very hilly, but the riverfront is flat and good for bike hire. There are bike hire outlets at Belém (see page 83) and Doca de Santo Amaro (Armazém 7 ☎ 218 250 266; daily 10am–7pm). Expect to pay around €5 an hour.

Children

Portugal is very child-friendly, and kids are welcome in most restaurants and cafés. While dedicated children's menus are rare, most restaurants will serve a half-portion (*meia dose*) of dishes from the menu. Beware that many of the streets are narrow, cobbled and steep, so can be awkward for pushchairs.

Cinemas

Mainstream **films** are shown at various multiplexes around the city, usually with Portuguese subtitles. Listings can be found on Ⓦ agendalx.pt. The Instituto da Cinemateca Portuguesa (Rua Barata Salgueiro 39 Ⓜ Avenida ☎ 213 596 200, Ⓦ cinemateca.pt), the national film theatre, has twice-daily shows and contains its own cinema museum.

Crime

Violent crime is very rare but pickpocketing is common, especially on public transport.

Disabilities

Lisbon airport offers a service for **wheelchair-users** if advance notice is given to your airline (details on Ⓦ ana.pt, ☎ 218 413 500), while the Orange Badge symbol is recognized for disabled car parking. The main public transport company, Carris, offers an inexpensive dial-a-ride minibus service, O Serviço Mobilidade Reduzida especial, (€1.80 per trip; Mon–Fri 6.30am–9.30pm, Sat & Sun 8am–noon & 2–6pm; ☎ 213 613 141, Ⓦ carris.pt), though two days' advance notice and a medical certificate are required.

Electricity

Portugal uses two-pin plugs (220/240v). UK appliances will work with a continental adaptor.

Embassies and consulates

Australia, Avenida da Liberdade 2002 Ⓜ Avenida; ☎ 213 101 500; Canada, Avenida da Liberdade 198–200–3° Ⓜ Avenida; ☎ 213 164 600; Ireland, Avenida da Liberdade 200–4° Ⓜ Avenida; ☎ 213 308 200; South Africa, Avda Luís Bivar 10 Ⓜ Picoas; ☎ 213 192 200; UK, Rua de São Bernardo 33 Ⓜ Rato; ☎ 213 924 000, Ⓦ www.gov.uk /world/portugal; US, Avenida das Forças Armadas, Ⓜ Jardim Zoológico; ☎ 217 273 300, Ⓦ pt. usembassy.gov.

Event listings

The best listings magazine is the free monthly *Agenda Cultural* (Ⓦ www. agendalx.pt) produced by the town hall (in Portuguese! *Follow me Lisboa* is an English-language version produced by the local tourist office. Both are available from the tourist offices and larger hotels.

Health

Pharmacies, the first point of call if you are ill, are open Mon–Fri 9am–1pm & 3–7pm, Sat 9am–1pm. Details of

Emergencies

For police, fire and ambulance services, dial ☏ 112

24hr pharmacies are posted on every pharmacy door, or call ☏ 118. The most central hospital is Hospital de Santa Maria (Avenida Prof. Egas Moniz ☏ 217 805 000, ⓦ chln.pt; Ⓜ Entre Campos). There are various other public hospitals around the city; EU citizens will need form E112.

Internet
Most hotels offer free wi-fi and often have computers for public use in reception. Most large cafés, bars and restaurants also offer free wi-fi.

Left luggage
There are 24hr lockers at the airport, main train and bus station, charging around €8 per day; for alternative venues around the city, check ⓦ bagbnb.com/luggage-storage/lisbon.

LGBTQ travellers
The Centro Comunitário Gay e Lésbico de Lisboa at Rua dos Fanqueieiros 40 (☏ 218 873 918; Wed– Sat 7–11pm; Ⓜ Martim Moniz) is the main gay and lesbian community centre, run by ILGA, whose website (ⓦ www.ilga-portugal. pt) is in Portuguese.

Lost property
Report any loss to the **tourist police** station in the Foz Cultura building in Palácio Foz, Praça dos Restauradores (daily 24hr ☏ 213 421 634). For items left on public transport, contact Carris ☏ 218 535 403.

Money
Portugal uses the **euro** (€). Banks open Monday to Friday 8.30am–3pm. Most central branches have automatic exchange machines for various currencies. You can withdraw up to €300 per day from ATMs ("Multibanco") with a maximum €200 per transaction – check fees with your home bank.

Opening hours
Most **shops** open Monday to Saturday 9am–7pm; smaller shops close for lunch (around 1–3pm) and on Saturday afternoons; shopping centres are open daily until 10pm or later. Most **museums** and **monuments** open Tuesday to Sunday from around 10am–6pm; details are given in the Guide.

Opera
Lisbon's main opera house is the Rococo Teatro Nacional São Carlos (Rua Serpa Pinto 9 ☏ 213 253 045, ⓦ tnsc.pt).

Phones
Most European-subscribed **mobile phones** will work in Lisbon, and those with mobiles from EU countries will pay no additional roaming charges.

Post
Post offices (*correios*) are usually open Monday to Friday 8.30am–6.30pm. The main Lisbon office at Praça dos Restauradores 58 is open until 10pm, and 9am–6pm on Sat (☏ 213 238 971). Stamps (*selos*) are sold at post offices and anywhere that has the sign "Correio de Portugal – Selos" displayed.

Smoking
In common with most other EU countries, smoking is prohibited in most restaurants and cafés.

Sports

Lisbon boasts two of Europe's top **football** teams (see page 98), Benfica (ⓦslbenfica.pt) and Sporting (ⓦsporting.pt). Fixtures and news on ⓦligaportugal.pt. The area also contains some of Europe's best **golf courses**, especially around Cascais and Estoril (info at ⓦwww.portugalgolf.pt). The Atlantic beaches at Caparica and Guincho are ideal for **surfing** and windsurfing, and international competitions are frequently held there (details on ⓦsurfingportugal.com). **Horseriding** is superb in the Sintra hills, and skilled horsemanship can also be seen at Portuguese **bullfights** (see Praça de Touros, page 97). The Estoril Open in April/May draws **tennis** fans to the city (ⓦmillenniumestorilopen.com), and thousands of runners hit the streets for the **Lisbon Marathon** (ⓦmaratonclubedeportugal.com), held in September/October.

Tickets

You can **buy tickets** for Lisbon's theatres and many concerts from the ticket desk in FNAC (ⓦbilheteira.fnac.pt) in the Armazéns do Chiado shopping centre (see page 54), as well as from the main venues themselves. Online tickets can be purchased from ⓦticketline.sapo.pt or ⓦblueticket.pt.

Time

Portuguese **time** is the same as Greenwich Mean Time (GMT). Clocks go forward an hour in late March and back to GMT in late October.

Tipping

Service charges are included in hotel and restaurant bills. A ten-percent tip is usual for restaurant bills, and hotel porters and toilet attendants expect at least €0.50.

Toilets

There are very few **public toilets** in the streets, although they can be found in nearly all main tourist sights (signed variously as *casa de banho, retrete, banheiro, lavabos* or "WC"), or sneak into a café or restaurant if need be. Gents are usually marked "H" (*homens*) or "C" (*cabalheiros*), and ladies "M" (*mulheres*) or "S" (*senhoras*).

Tourist information

Lisbon's main **tourist office** is the Lisbon Welcome Centre at Praça do Comércio (see map on p.26; daily 9am–8pm; ☏ 210 312 810, ⓦvisitlisboa.com), which can supply accommodation lists, bus timetables and maps. The main Portugal tourist office at Palácio Foz, Praça dos Restauradores (daily 9am–8pm; ☏ 213 463 314), is also helpful.

Tourist offices at the airport (see page 136) and at Santa Apolónia station (Tues–Sat 7.30am–9.30pm; ☏ 910 517 982) can help you find accommodation, as can a few smaller "Ask Me" kiosks dotted around town, like the one opposite Belém's Mosteiro dos Jerónimos (daily 9am–6pm). There is also the Y Lisboa tourist office at Rua Jardim do Regedor 50 (daily 10am–8pm; ☏ 213 472 134), with information geared to young and student travellers.

There are also tourist offices in all the main **day-trip destinations**: Sintra Turismo (see map, p.110; daily 9.30am–6pm, until 7pm in August; ☏ 219 231 157, ⓦcm-sintra.pt/turismo); Cascais Turismo (Praça 5 de Outubro; daily 9am–6pm; open til 8pm in summer; ☏ 912 034 214, ⓦvisitcascais.com); and Caparica Turismo (Frente Urbana de Praias; Mon–Sat 9.30am–1pm & 2–5.30pm, closed Sat from Oct–March; ☏ 212 900 071, ⓦwww.m-almada.pt).

Travel agents

The well-informed Top Atlântico, Rua do Ouro 109 (☎ 213 403 220, ⓦ topatlantico.pt), Baixa, also acts as an American Express agent.

Water

Lisbon's **water** is technically safe to drink, though you may prefer bottled water. Inexpensive bottled water is sold in any supermarket, though tourist shops and restaurants charge considerably more.

Festivals and events

Carnival

February–March
Brazilian-style parades and costumes, mainly at Parque das Nações.

Peixe em Lisboa

March–April
ⓦ www.peixemlisboa.com
Lisbon's annual fish festival takes place in Parque Eduardo VII and includes masterclasses by top chefs.

Sintra Music Festival

May ⓦ festivaldesintra.pt
Performances by international orchestras and dance groups in and around Sintra, Estoril and Cascais.

Rock in Rio Lisboa

May (even yearly)
ⓦ rockinriolisboa.sapo.pt
Five-day mega rock festival in Parque Bela Vista, in the north of the city.

Santos Populares

June
June sees a series of city-wide events loosely based around three saints' days.

Lisbon's main festival is for its adopted saint, Santo António. On June 12 there's a parade down Avenida da Liberdade followed by a giant street party in the Alfama, and the whole city is decked out in coloured ribbons with pots of lucky basil placed on window sills.

Lisboa Pride

June/July ⓦ ilga-portugal.pt
Lisbon's increasingly popular LGBTQ Pride changes venues, but in recent years has been held at Praça do Comércio.

Superbock Superrock

July ⓦ superbocksuperrock.pt
One of the country's largest rock festivals, with local and international bands at Parque das Nações and other venues.

NOS Alive

July ⓦ nosalive.com
Another big-time rock festival at the Passeio Marítimo de Algés, on the riverfront west of Belém, attracting big-name acts.

Public holidays

In addition to Christmas (Dec 24–25) and New Year's Day public holidays include Shrove Tuesday (Feb/March); Good Friday (March/April); April 25 (Liberty Day); May 1 (Labour Day); Corpus Christi (late May/early June); June 10 (Portugal/Camões Day); June 12 (Santo António); Feast of the Assumption (Aug 15); Republic Day (Oct 5); All Saint's Day (Nov 1); Independence Day (Dec 1); Immaculate Conception (Dec 8).

Jazz em Augusto

August Ⓦ **musica.gulbenkian.pt**
Big annual (Jazz in August) festival at the Gulbenkian's open-air amphitheatre.

Christmas (natal)

The main Christmas celebration is midnight Mass on December 24, which is followed by a meal of *bacalhau*.

New Year's Eve (ano novo)

The best place for New Year's Eve is Praça do Comércio, where fireworks light up the riverfront, while the New Year's Day swim at Carcavelos Beach is a popular hangover cure.

Chronology

60 BC Julius Caesar establishes Olisipo as the capital of the Roman Empire's western colony.

711 Moors from North Africa conquer Iberia, building a fortress by the *alhama* (hot springs), now known as Alfama.

1147 Afonso Henriques, the first king of the newly established Portuguese state, retakes Lisbon from the Moors and builds a cathedral on the site of the former mosque.

1495–1521 The reign of Dom Manuel I coincides with the golden age of Portuguese exploration. So-called "Manueline" architecture celebrates the opening of sea routes. The 1494 Treaty of Tordesillas gives Spain and Portugal trading rights to much of the globe.

1498 Vasco da Gama returns to Belém with spices from India, which helps fund the building of the monastery of Jerónimos.

1581 Victorious after the battle of Alcántara, Philip II of Spain becomes Filipe I of Portugal, and Portugal loses its independence.

1640 Portuguese conspirators storm the palace in Lisbon and install the Duke of Bragança as João IV, ending Spanish rule.

1706–50 Under João V, gold and diamonds from Brazil kick-start a second golden age; lavish building programmes include the Aqueduto das Águas Livres.

1755 The Great Earthquake flattens much of Lisbon. The Baixa is rebuilt in "Pombaline" style, named after the Marquês de Pombal.

1800s Maria II (1843–53) rules with German consort, Fernando II, and establishes the palaces at Ajuda and Pena in Sintra. Fado becomes popular in the Alfama. Avenida da Liberdade is laid out.

1900–10 Carlos I is assassinated in Lisbon in 1908, while two years later, the exile of Manuel II marks the end of the monarchy and birth of the Republic.

1932–68 Salazar's dictatorship sees development stagnate. Despite massive rural poverty, elaborate "New State" architecture includes the Ponte 25 de Abril, originally named Ponte de Salazar.

1974 April 25 marks a largely peaceful Revolution. Former Portuguese colonies are granted independence, leading to large-scale immigration.

1986 Entry to the European Community enables a rapid redevelopment of Lisbon.

1990s Lisbon's role as Capital of Culture (1994) and host of Expo '98 helps fund a metro extension, the Ponte Vasco da Gama and the Parque das Nações.

2000–05 In 2004 Lisbon hosts the European Football Championships. Fado star Mariza brings the music to an international audience.

2005–2015 EU leaders sign the Lisbon Treaty on Dec 13, 2007, agreeing a draft constitution. Ten new upmarket hotels open in 2014, adding to Lisbon's burgeoning hotel scene.

2016 Socialist António Costa wins a controversial election with the support of the Communist party, vowing to "turn the page on austerity".

2018 Lisbon's Altice Arena hosts the Eurovision Song Contest, boosting an already record-high number of visitors to the city.

Portuguese

English is widely spoken in most of Lisbon's hotels and tourist restaurants, but you will find a few words of Portuguese extremely useful. Written Portuguese is similar to Spanish, though pronunciation is very different. Vowels are often nasal or ignored altogether. The consonants are, at least, consistent:

Consonants

c is soft before e and i, hard otherwise unless it has a cedilla – *açucar* (sugar) is pronounced "assookar".

ch is somewhat softer than in English; *chá* (tea) sounds like Shah.

j is like the "s" in pleasure, as is g except when it comes before a "hard" vowel (a, o and u).

lh sounds like "lyuh".

q is always pronounced as a "k".

s before a consonant or at the end of a word becomes "sh", otherwise it's as in English – Cascais is pronounced "Kashkaish".

x is also pronounced "sh"– Baixa is pronounced "Baisha".

Vowels

e/é: e at the end of a word is silent unless it has an accent, so that *carne* (meat) is pronounced "karn", while *café* is "caf-ay".

ã or õ: the tilde renders the pronunciation much like the French -an and -on endings, only more nasal.

ão: this sounds something like a strangled "Ow!" cut off in midstream (as in *pão*, bread – *são*, saint – *limão*, lemon).

ei: this sounds like "ay" (as in *feito* – finished)

ou: this sounds like "oh" (as in *roupa* – clothes)

Words and phrases

Basics

sim yes
não no
olá hello
bom dia good morning
boa tarde/noite good afternoon/night
adeus goodbye
até logo see you later
hoje today
amanhã tomorrow
por favor/se faz favor please
tudo bem? everything all right?
está bem it's all right/OK
obrigado/a thank you (male/ female speaker)
onde where
que what
quando when
porquê why
como how
quanto how much
não sei I don't know
sabe...? do you know...?
pode...? could you...?
há...? (silent "h") is there...? there is
tem...? (pron. "taying") do you have...?
queria... I'd like...

desculpe sorry
com licença excuse me
fala Inglês? do you speak English?
não compreendo I don't understand
este/a this
esse/a that
agora now
mais tarde later
mais more
menos less
grande big
pequeno little
aberto open
fechado closed
senhoras women
homens men
lavabo/quarto de banho toilet/bathroom

Getting around

esquerda left
direita right
sempre em frente straight ahead
aqui here
ali there
perto near
longe far
Onde é... Where is ...
 a estação de camionetas? the bus station?
 a paragem de autocarro para... the bus stop for...
Donde parte o autocarro para...? Where does the bus to...leave from?
A que horas parte? (chega a...?) What time does it leave? (arrive at...?)
Pare aqui por favor Stop here please
bilhete (para) ticket (to)
ida e volta round trip

Common signs

aberto open
fechado closed
entrada entrance
saída exit
puxe pull
empurre push
elevador lift
pré-pagamento pay in advance
perigo/perigoso danger/ous
proibido estacionar no parking
obras (road) works

Accommodation

Queria um quarto I'd like a room
É para uma noite (semana) It's for one night (week)
É para uma pessoa (duas pessoas) It's for one person/two people
Quanto custa? How much is it?
Posso ver? May I see/ look?
Há um quarto mais barato? Is there a cheaper room?
com duche with a shower

Shopping

Quanto é? How much is it?
banco; câmbio bank; change
correios post office
(dois) selos (two) stamps
Como se diz isto em Português? What's this called in Portuguese?
O que é isso? What's that?
saldo sale
esgotado sold out

Days of the week

Domingo Sunday
Segunda-feira Monday
Terça-feira Tuesday
Quarta-feira Wednesday
Quinta-feira Thursday
Sexta-feira Friday
Sábado Saturday

Months

Janeiro January
Fevereiro February
Março March
Abril April
Maio May
Junho June
Julho July
Agosto August
Aetembro September
Outubro October
Novembro November
Dezembro December

Useful words

azulejo glazed, painted tile
cais quay
capela chapel

PORTUGUESE

casa house
centro comercial shopping centre
estação station
estrada/rua street/road
feira fair or market
igreja church
jardim garden
miradouro viewpoint/belvedere
praça/largo square

Numbers

um/uma 1
dois/duas 2
três 3
quatro 4
cinco 5
seis 6
sete 7
oito 8
nove 9
dez 10
onze 11
doze 12
treze 13
catorze 14
quinze 15
dezasseis 16
dezasete 17
dezoito 18
dezanove 19
vinte 20
vinte e um 21
trinta 30
quarenta 40
cinquenta 50
sessenta 60
setenta 70
oitenta 80
noventa 90
cem 100
cento e um 101
duzentos 200
quinhentos 500
mil 1000

Food and drink terms

Basics

assado roasted
colher spoon
conta bill
copo glass
cozido boiled
ementa menu
estrelado/frito fried
faca knife
garfo fork
garrafa bottle
grelhado grilled
mexido scrambled

Menu terms

pequeno almoço breakfast
almoço lunch
jantar dinner
ementa turística set menu
prato do dia dish of the day
especialidades speciality
lista de vinhos wine list
entradas starters
petiscos snacks
sobremesa dessert

Soups, salad and staples

açucár sugar
arroz rice
azeitonas olives
batatas fritas chips/french fries
caldo verde cabbage soup
fruta fruit
legumes vegetables
manteiga butter
massa pasta
molho (de tomate/piri-piri) tomato/chilli sauce
omeleta omelette
ovos eggs
pão bread
pimenta pepper
piri-piri chilli sauce
queijo cheese
sal salt
salada salad
sopa de legumes vegetable soup
sopa de marisco shellfish soup
sopa de peixe fish soup

Fish and shellfish

atum tuna
camarões shrimp

carapau mackerel
cherne stone bass
dourada bream
espada scabbard fish
espadarte swordfish
gambas prawns
lagosta lobster
lulas (grelhadas) squid (grilled)
mexilhões mussels
pescada hake
polvo octopus
robalo sea bass
salmão salmon
salmonete red mullet
santola spider crab
sapateira crab
sardinhas sardines
tamboril monkfish
truta trout
viera scallop

Meat

alheira chicken sausage
borrego lamb
chanfana lamb or goat casserole
chouriço spicy sausage
coelho rabbit
cordeiro lamb
dobrada/tripa tripe
espetada mista mixed meat kebab
febras pork steaks
fiambre ham
fígado liver
frango no churrasco barbecued chicken
leitão roast suckling pig
pato duck
perdiz partridge
perú turkey
picanha strips of beef in garlic sauce
presunto smoked ham
rim kidney
rodizio barbecued meats
rojões cubed pork cooked in blood with
potatoes
vitela veal

portuguese specialities

açorda bread-based stew (often seafood)
arroz de marisco seafood rice
bacalhau à brás salted cod with egg and
potatoes
bacalhau a Gomes Sá dried cod baked with
potatoes,
bacalhau na brasa dried cod roasted with
potatoes egg and olives
bife à portuguesa thin beef steak with a
fried egg on top
caldeirada fish stew
cataplana fish, shellfish or meat stewed in a
circular metal dish
cozido à portuguesa boiled casserole
of meat and beans, served with rice and
vegetables
feijoada bean stew with meat and
vegetables
migas meat or fish in a bready garlic sauce
porco à alentejana pork cooked withclams

snacks and desserts

arroz doce rice pudding
bifana steak sandwich
bolo cake
gelado ice cream
pastéis de bacalhau dried cod cakes
pastel de nata custard tart
prego steak sandwich
pudim crème caramel

Drinks

um copo/uma garrafa de/da... a glass/
bottle of...
vinho branco/tinto white/red wine
cerveja beer
água (sem/com gás) mineral water
(without/with gas)
fresca/natural chilled/room temperature
sumo de laranja/maçã orange/apple juice
chá tea
café coffee
sem/com leite without/with milk
sem/com açúcar without/with sugar

SMALL PRINT

Publishing Information
Fifth edition 2019

Distribution
UK, Ireland and Europe
Apa Publications (UK) Ltd; sales@roughguides.com
United States and Canada
Ingram Publisher Services; ips@ingramcontent.com
Australia and New Zealand
Woodslane; info@woodslane.com.au
Southeast Asia
Apa Publications (SN) Pte; sales@roughguides.com
Worldwide
Apa Publications (UK) Ltd; sales@roughguides.com

Special Sales, Content Licensing and CoPublishing
Rough Guides can be purchased in bulk quantities at discounted prices. We can create special editions, personalised jackets and corporate imprints tailored to your needs. sales@roughguides.com.
roughguides.com
Printed in China by RR Donnelley Asia Printing Solutions Limited

Rough Guide Credits
Editor: Joanna Reeves
Cartography: Ed Wright
Managing editor: Rachel Lawrence
Picture editor: Aude Vauconsant
Cover photo research: Tom Smyth

Original design: Richard Czapnik
Senior DTP coordinator: Dan May
Head of DTP and Pre-Press: Rebeka Davies

Author: Matthew Hancock fell in love with Portugal when he was a teacher in Lisbon. He later returned to the country to walk the 775-mile Portuguese-Spanish border. Now a journalist and editor living in Dorset, he is also the author of the Rough Guides to the Algarve, Madeira and Porto and co-author of the Rough Guide to Portugal and the Rough Guide to Dorset, Hampshire and the Isle of Wight. He also contributes to the Rough Guides to England, Britain and Spain. With additional accounts by Amanda Tomlin.

Acknowledgements

Thanks to everyone who helped, especially Vitor Carriço at Visit Lisbon, Heritage and Almalusa Hotels, Luke Tilley, Alex and Olivia and especially Amanda Tomlin. Thanks too to everyone at Rough Guides, especially Joanna Reeves for her helpful editing.

Help us update

We've gone to a lot of effort to ensure that this edition of the **Pocket Rough Guide Lisbon** is accurate and up-to-date. However, things change – places get "discovered", opening hours are notoriously fickle, restaurants and rooms raise prices or lower standards. If you feel we've got it wrong or left something out, we'd like to know, and if you can remember the address, the price, the hours, the phone number, so much the better.

Please send your comments with the subject line "**Pocket Rough Guide Lisbon Update**" to mail@uk.roughguides.com. We'll credit all contributions and send a copy of the next edition (or any other Rough Guide if you prefer) for the very best emails.

Photo Credits

(Key: T-top; C-centre; B-bottom; L-left; R-right)

Index

NOTES

NOTES